THE FEMINIST REVOLUTION

Susan B. Anthony 1820–1906
"Women have been taught always to work for something else than their own personal freedom."

Margaret Sanger 1879–1966
In *The Woman Rebel,* Sanger offered specific information on birth control for girls aged fourteen to eighteen: "In this present chaos of sex atmosphere, it is difficult to know just what to do, or really what constitutes clean living without prudishness."

Betty Friedan 1921–2006
Friedan wrote the purpose of the National Organization for Women (NOW) on a paper napkin: "To take the actions needed to bring women into the mainstream of American society, now; full equality for women, in fully equal partnership with men."

Jules Archer History
for Young Readers

THE FEMINIST REVOLUTION

A STORY OF THE THREE MOST INSPIRING AND EMPOWERING WOMEN IN AMERICAN HISTORY: SUSAN B. ANTHONY, MARGARET SANGER, AND BETTY FRIEDAN

JULES ARCHER

Foreword by Naomi Wolf

Sky Pony Press
NEW YORK

Historical texts often reflect the time period in which they were written, and new information is constantly being discovered. This book was originally published in 1975, and much has changed since then. While every effort has been made to bring this book up to date, it is important to consult multiple sources when doing research.

To Susan B. Anthony, Margaret Sanger, and Betty Friedan for their passionate dedication to the liberation of women

CONTENTS

FOREWORD

It is impossible to overstress the role that is played in female consciousness by all the influential women in history, both those who we remember and those who we have forgotten.

I found this to be true in my own life. When I was a student at Oxford in the 1980s, women had only recently been admitted to most colleges. But even though we made our (numerically unequal) appearances, our reading lists of great writers and great books were overwhelmingly male. Our professors were male— feminist theory and history scarcely existed as a discipline—and even the portraits on the ancient walls were all of men, and had been for over six hundred years. The way recorders of history omitted these women from history itself profoundly affected me as a female student: It was difficult to imagine my own possible place in the canon as a female writer, and it was even more difficult for me to see my own potential and that of my female friends, since the histories we read were of male leaders or male-dominated, world changing events, such as the outcomes of wars. Most of the relevant information about women in the period which I was studying—the nineteenth and twentieth centuries— as well as that of significant women leaders and influencers in general, simply went unrecorded and untaught.

Thirty years later, the fact that feminist historians and critics have "won" many major battles about what gets written into history, and who gets included, has changed the landscape for students—indeed for us all—in a new way. The way we teach history today has much more dimension, and reflects more accurately the lives and material conditions of real people. The literary canon is much more diverse, and female students studying literature no longer feel the same sense of exclusion that we once did.

The lives of the women narrated in this collection of biographies outline an important part of history that should not be overlooked. Each of these women leaders greatly affected and changed the period in which they lived. Each biography reflects the unique social conditions that made or limited women's opportunities during these women's lives. In the stories of Susan B. Anthony, Margaret Sanger, and Betty Friedan, you can also see reflected in very detailed ways, in very concrete options and possibilities available to each of these women, the progress of feminism.

A life that reflects her time in American history, and one that also shows the importance of reading about the lives of influential women alongside the larger familiar narrative of US history, is that of Susan B. Anthony. Her origin as the daughter of a Quaker community reflects the rise and influence of the Great Awakenings following religious revivals in the earlier decades of the nineteenth century. That religious-inspired, reformist energy eventually contributed to the rise of the Abolitionist movement in the 1840s through the early 1860s and up to the Civil War. Their anti-slavery movement was a vast and transformational movement that split American society. Anthony received her activist start as an abolitionist, but after she was rejected from speaking at an anti-slavery forum, she began to fight for women's rights. The antislavery arguments in that era, of course, helped inevitably to lay the groundwork for First Wave feminism. If slaves were entitled to basic civil rights and equality, how could a feminist argument along a similar structure not follow? Anthony's later career leading the First Wave of feminism and the fight for women's voting rights reflected how the struggle for voting rights was the paramount focus of reformist energies for both of these movements, abolitionist and feminist. Anthony's skill at building coalitions and pressuring existing political parties and legislatures lay the foundation for one of the most important events in history: the signing of the Nineteenth Amendment in 1920. Her sixty-year struggle for American women's voting rights, and the many roadblocks she encountered along the way, have enduring lessons for us regarding how important the law and Constitution are when it comes to issues of advocacy in a democratic society. Her uphill battle also tells us a great deal about the perils of activism and the kinds of opposition a society can mount against a really challenging reformer. Her biography has lessons for us today that are as fresh and relevant as they were for her own generation and for the generation that followed hers, which saw the work she set in motion come to fruition through women becoming full citizens with the right to vote.

Fast forward to the work of Margaret Sanger: you see the endpoint of sixty years of First Wave feminist agitation. Sanger's generation inherited the benefits of the long struggle in Britain and in America for women's voting rights; by 1910 and 1920, educated women who had served in the war effort were reluctant to return home and devote themselves to a purely domestic life. The limited job options available, such as domestic workers, housewives, and shopgirls, were no longer appealing positions for working-class women. Colleges for women such as Smith, Barnard, and Vassar in America, and Girton College, Cambridge, and St Hilda's College, Oxford, in Britain, had been established. And women of all classes not only wanted, but also felt that they deserved, information about their own bodies and sexual health. Sanger was a pioneer who pushed the boundaries surrounding these issues. During her lifetime, she played a vital role in establishing clinics that distributed both contraceptive items and information about sexual health, and wrote many books about the same subjects. Her work in turn empowered the next two generations.

And that is where we see Betty Friedan's life come onto the stage. Friedan's peers inherited the rights earned by First

Wave feminism of the 1860s–1920, along with the practical accomplishments of Sanger's generation. Friedan's peers grew up with access to contraception and took for granted that they were entitled to be informed about their own bodies. They grew up expecting to vote, to drive, to have their own money, and perhaps even to work in one of many interesting fields that were opening up to women. By the 1950s, however, there was a backlash from social norms; popular opinion sought to send educated women back into a role of "mere" homemaker. Women in America had been working as diplomats and congresspeople, doctors and lawyers—though this was the exception rather than the rule. Some colleges had been coeducational for decades. As a result it was inevitable for an educated young woman such as Betty Friedan to look around at her life and ask: "Is this all there is?" The problem—one which Betty Friedan called "the problem with no name"—is that even though women in Margaret Sanger's generation fought for women's rights and gained many new privileges, women still were not granted the same rights as men. Once Friedan identified this problem, she ushered us into The Second Wave of Feminism, which we are living in today.

So does this mean that the battle is over? Of course not—social justice battles never end. The new issues that young feminists—many younger feminists call themselves Third and even Fourth Wave feminists—will have to tackle include the globalization of women's struggles, and the need for more globalized and localized analysis of women's problems; the continued fight to seriously investigate and punish sex crimes and gender-based violence; and the need to close the wage gap and make sure that top leadership positions in politics and business are gender balanced (currently women still only make up 5 to 10 percent of leadership positions). But young women— and young men—today inherit a much fairer world than did Friedan's generation, directly because of these two centuries of feminist struggle. Young people of both genders are much more aware of gender inequities; young men care as much about social justice and gender-based justice as young women do. We know better now that feminism is everyone's fight, and not just that of women. Many more young women around the world believe that they should have the right to tackle any task they wish to and technology is opening up opportunities that can transcend cultural biases against women and girls. It is an exciting time to be female because we have gained so much from the battles of the women detailed in the following pages.

But in order for you to become a leader who advocates even more fairness, justice, and equality for all, it is really important for you to know and understand history, to know what happened, and how things were for women—before female leaders of the past, such as Susan B. Anthony, Margaret Sanger, and Betty Friedan, made so many of the changes that now support and enrich our own lives.

—Dr. Naomi Wolf, bestselling author of *The Beauty Myth* and former political consultant for President Bill Clinton

INTRODUCTION

Greater recognition needs to be accorded women's role in, and contribution to, the American system. Significantly, a study reported in *The Historian: A Journal of History* found that 44 percent of general American history books do not even mention the struggle for woman suffrage, and 65 percent fail to record the name of Susan B. Anthony. Even more ignore the names of Margaret Sanger and Betty Friedan. As far as most of these books are concerned, women are invisible in American history.

This book explores the history of an idea essential to our times through the lives of the people most important to the development of that idea. The three women who did the most to advance the women's movement for sexual equality in America were Susan B. Anthony, Margaret Sanger, and Betty Friedan. Each dared defy convention, at great personal risk, in the cause of liberating women from the restrictions of a world controlled by men.

Each figured in a different stage of the women's movement. Susan B. Anthony, 1820–1906, was primarily responsible for winning the vote for women, giving them an equal say with men as to who represents their interests in the American system of government.

Margaret Sanger, 1879–1966, was the leading figure in the struggle of women to win control of their own bodies through the right to family planning. Sanger even went to prison to establish legal and public acceptance of birth control.

Betty Friedan, born in 1921, was primarily responsible for the modern movement known as women's liberation. She fought to win equality with men in society and under the law. It was Friedan who taught women to refuse to accept the limiting image of womanhood imposed upon them by male-dominated media, laws, and religious institutions, and to demand their full rights as human beings, workers, and citizens.

The conspicuous omission of these women is a glaring oversight in most history texts. By the failure to narrate the accomplishments of such women, these texts give students only an incomplete, male-oriented version of our history. They give the impression that the only people who contributed to the America we know were men.

It is the purpose of this book, and others to follow in this series, to open up new ways of looking at our history.

—Jules Archer
Santa Cruz, California

The Feminist Revolution

ONE

The American women's movement arose when a handful of determined women publicly demanded equality of opportunity and rights with men, long denied them. They challenged the male-imposed concept that women's proper role was in subservience to men.

Women's unequal status dated from primitive societies in which men were the warriors. Women were, in effect, their slaves, relegated to growing food, preparing meals, raising children, submitting to sexual advances, and caring for the sick and elderly.

Ancient religious systems around the world upheld, in one form or another, the East Indian edict: "Day and night must women be held by their protectors in a state of dependence."

In Western countries, the Bible was cited to support this practice as God-ordained:

> "Saint Paul said . . . and the head of every woman is man. . . . Let your women be silent in the churches, for it is not permitted unto them to speak. . . . And if they will learn anything, let them ask their husbands at home: for it is a shame for women to speak in the church. . . . But I suffer not a woman to teach, nor to usurp authority over the man, but to be in silence: for Adam was first formed, then Eve. . . . Saint Peter said: likewise, ye wives, be in subjection to your husbands." One medieval version of the Bible even declared that a husband with a balky wife had the right to "beate the feare of God into her head."

Yet, early on, women's rights had a few staunch male defenders. Among the ancient Greeks, the philosopher Plato and the dramatist Euripides urged equality for women. Greek satirist Aristophanes suggested in his play *Lysistrata* that women should

3

band together and refuse to sleep with their husbands until the men agreed to stop going to war.

In the fifteenth century, Christine de Pisan challenged man-made laws and attitudes that decreed women were men's property to do with as they wished. In the next century, English statesman Sir Thomas More championed women's rights.

One important early feminist was England's Mary Wollstonecraft. In her 1791 book, *Vindication for the Rights of Women,* she declared, "It is time to restore women to their lost dignity and to make them part of the human race." Her book was widely read in Europe and America, strongly influencing feminists who came after her.

Most countries' laws, however, were drawn by men to favor men. Women were denied many rights reserved for their husbands, fathers, and sons. Before the middle of the nineteenth century, women were barred from participating in politics, except in monarchies as hereditary queens or noblewomen.

One of the earliest American women rebels was Abigail Adams, wife of President John Adams. When he was at the Continental Congress planning for a new American republic, she wrote him urging that he make sure the new code of laws forbade husbands unlimited power over wives. Because, she said, "all men would be tyrants if they could." Wasn't that, in fact, the very reason the colonies were fighting England? "If particular care and attention is not paid to the Ladies," Abigail warned, "we are determined to foment a Rebellion, and will not hold ourselves bound by any laws in which we have no voice or Representatives."

In the first part of the nineteenth century, only boys were allowed to attend free American high schools. Girls were not permitted to study such "manly" subjects as math and science. In 1821, educator Emma Willard defied these taboos by founding the Troy Female Seminary in New York State, giving girls a free high school education equal to that of boys.

The first American woman to speak out effectively in public for women's rights was Frances Wright, a Scottish-American reformer. Pioneering as a woman lecturer in 1833, she advocated equal education for women. "Unless women assume the place in society which good sense and good feeling alike assign to them," she declared, "human improvement must advance but feebly." She spoke to working men as well as women all over the country.

Thanks to her influence, Mt. Holyoke was founded in 1837 to give women their first chance at a college education equal to a man's. Nevertheless, the Victorian insistence on female inferiority, so soothing to male vanity, persisted throughout the century.

According to Victorian-era scientists, women were by nature inferior to men. The shape and size of their skulls allegedly indicated weaker brainpower. They were also presumed to have a slower metabolism, causing lower vitality. And the process of menstruation was judged to be so debilitating as to make the very condition of being a woman a form of disease.

TWO

Women were allowed their first opportunity to band together in 1837 when they attended the first national antislavery convention in New York. The abolitionist movement made women's public participation in a political cause respectable. Prominent among these feminist abolitionists were Lucy Stone, Angelina and Sarah Grimké, Lucretia Mott, Elizabeth Cady Stanton, and Susan B. Anthony.

From women's struggle to free the slaves, it was only one more step to mount another struggle to free themselves from male domination. The germ of this crusade was planted in 1840 when Mott and Stanton, along with other American delegates, attended a World Anti-Slavery Convention in London.

The male-dominated convention voted to seat only male delegates. In Britain, as in the US, there was a distinct prejudice against the "unladylike" idea of public speaking by women, who were supposed to leave that to men.

Humiliated by being relegated to the nonparticipating galleries for ten days, Mott and Stanton angrily vowed to fight for women's right to full equality with men.

In 1848, they organized the first Women's Rights Convention at Seneca Falls, New York. Delegates demanded not only woman suffrage, but equality for wives, who were placed in virtual subjugation to their husbands under civil law.

Noted male abolitionists supported the feminists who signed a Declaration of Independence for Women. But newspapers and clergymen blasted the women rebels with such fiery denunciations and ridicule that the more fainthearted recanted.

Religious male chauvinists insisted that men were the obviously superior sex because Jesus Christ was a man, while Eve, the first woman, was a sinner who had caused Adam's fall. Equal rights for women were also disputed because, if granted, they would "destroy the femininity of women, who depend upon the strength, assistance, and gallantry of men."

Male champions of chivalry, however, raised no objections to the employment of working-class and black women in hard and dangerous physical labor. Their hypocrisy was exposed in 1851 at a Women's Rights Convention in Akron, Ohio, by a freed black slave woman who called herself Sojourner Truth. When a clergyman in the audience protested that women were too weak and helpless to be allowed to vote, Sojourner rose to respond.

"The man over there," she stated, "says women need to be helped into carriages and lifted over ditches, and have the best places everywhere. Nobody ever helps *me* into carriages or over puddles, or gives me the best place—and ain't I a woman? Look at my arm! I have ploughed and planted and gathered into barns, and no man could head me—and ain't I a woman? I could work as much and eat as much as a man—when I could get it—and bear the lash as well. And ain't I a woman?"

Feminists created an uproar in 1851 when they adopted a new dress style introduced by Mrs. Elizabeth Smith Miller. It was popularized by Mrs. Amelia Jenks Bloomer, after whom the new costume was named—"bloomers." Instead of the modest, cumbersome, all-concealing hoopskirt, the lower half of the feminists' legs was clad in full Turkish trousers gathered at the ankles.

It was as if they were calling the world's attention to the shocking fact that beneath their voluminous hoop-skirts, women actually walked on two legs—like men!—and didn't glide on wheels or rollers. The bloomers made it easier for women to get in and out of doorways, carriages, and trains; to get through rainy and muddy streets; to walk through country lanes; and to do housework.

The feminists eventually felt compelled to abandon the bloomers, however, because their dress rather than their message was getting all the public attention and comment. Nevertheless, this early revolt against traditional female attire eventually freed all women to choose the clothing they preferred.

The door to the professions was pushed open for women by the first woman doctor, Elizabeth Blackwell. She forced her way into one medical school after being rejected by twenty-nine others. Enduring taunts and insults from the male students, she graduated at the head of her class, winning her MD in 1849. However, no patients would consult, and no hospitals admit to practice, America's first woman doctor. So she opened the New York Infirmary in 1857 with an all-woman staff. Subsequently, she established medical schools for women.

Dr. Blackwell inspired another woman, slender, frail Mary Walker, to fight her way into medical school and win her MD When the Civil War broke out, she wrote her father, "Here is my chance to show the women of America what can be done by our sex in an affair which has always been considered men's business—war. I intend to volunteer for medical service with the Union Army. They will not dare to turn down a physician, woman or not!"

She put on trousers to become the first woman to serve on a modern battlefield. "We will be treated as equals," she wrote Amelia Bloomer, "only when we dispense with the nonsense of disguising our bodies by wires, bones, buttons, pads, stays, and stuffings."

To aid wounded soldiers, Dr. Walker often risked flying shot and shell. Her service was so brave and distinguished that Congress awarded her the Congressional Medal of Honor for exceptional valor. Having shown the nation what a woman in trousers could do, she then became a one-woman lobby for a proposed bill to equalize the rights of the sexes. She fought for it persistently for fifty-four years until her death in 1919.

THREE

Under the leadership of Susan B. Anthony, feminists continually pressed for full equality with men, including the right to vote. But the majority of American women were reluctant to support their efforts to change the status quo.

In 1870, a typical letter to the editor of the *Santa Cruz Sentinel,* signed by "A California Woman," protested, "Is it proper for women to mingle in politics and expose themselves to the polls as objects for the vulgar crowd to pass censorious remarks upon? . . . Let every sound-minded woman be satisfied with their home and strive to make it as attractive as possible."

A feminist named Georgianna Kirby replied to her: "In our eyes it is more praiseworthy for women to be out in the world, earning an honest living for her family and bringing up her children in a genial atmosphere of a cheerful, comfortable home. The woman imprisoned for life within the four walls of her kitchen becomes a drudge and in nine cases out of ten, a slave to a coarse and brutal husband. . . . The domestic slave is miserable unto death and is referred to as a gem of a wife."

The male prejudice against women was never more clearly evidenced than in an 1879 editorial in the *Richmond Herald.* "There is not a man in this whole land," it declared unequivocally, "who wouldn't rather have a boy baby than a girl baby any time."

Yet there were scattered pockets of males in progressive communities who supported the feminists. In Santa Cruz, women were granted suffrage in 1896 by a male vote, fifteen years before the state, and twenty-four years ahead of the rest of the country.

The struggle for equal rights originated mostly with middle-class women who had the time and money to write and publish tracts, organize feminist societies, and put pressure on legislators for both the vote and equal rights before the law.

One feminist exception was Margaret Sanger, who came from a poor, lower-class background. Her awareness of the suffering of poor women condemned to continual unwanted childbirth led her to campaign for legal birth control clinics. Breaking the law to help these women, she endured jail and great hardships until she was finally able to achieve her goal.

In 1907, Alice Paul, an American Quaker studying in England, joined English campaigns for woman suffrage. Arrested and jailed three times, she went on a hunger strike and was forcibly fed. She returned home to join Carrie Chapman Catt's National American Woman Suffrage Association, which at its peak had two million paid members.

In 1913, Paul organized a group later known as the National Woman's Party, which used radical tactics to campaign for the vote. Catt's organization disowned the Paul group for insisting upon petitioning Congress and the Wilson administration, instead of individual state governments. When Paul's suffragettes marched up Pennsylvania Avenue in Washington in 1913, their parade was disrupted by a jeering mob.

After World War I began, suffragettes chained themselves to the White House fence. Arrested, they went on hunger strikes in jail, and made more headlines when they were force-fed by police. Women's right to the vote was reinforced by their war effort, substituting for men called to uniform in factories, offices, and public jobs. Arguing that women were proving themselves the equals of men in both work and patriotic service, suffragettes demanded the vote as fully participating citizens.

On January 10, 1918, the Nineteenth Amendment, giving women the right to vote and known as the Susan Anthony Amendment in her honor, was introduced into the House of Representatives. After the war, on August 26, 1920, it was finally ratified into law.

Not satisfied with that victory, Paul pressed her campaign for another amendment to guarantee total equality between men and women in every aspect of American life. The US Women's Bureau, organized in 1920 under the Department of Labor, accused the Woman's Party of "a kind of hysterical feminism with a slogan for a program." Paul continued to fight for the Equal Rights Amendment until her death at age ninety-two in 1977.

The ERA was first introduced in Congress as early as 1923 by Representative Daniel Anthony, Susan Anthony's nephew. It eventually passed in 1972, but failed to get the necessary states' votes for ratification as a constitutional amendment.

When World War II broke out, women once more flocked into industry to take the place of men called to arms. "Rosie the Riveter" became a popular song of the day, memorializing this change in society's structure. After the war, women increasingly entered the workplace, out of choice or necessity, but the higher positions and higher salaries were limited to men.

The women's movement fell largely apathetic until 1953, when French author Simone de Beauvoir stirred international attention with a book titled *The Second Sex*. In it, she claimed all the countries of the world were male-dominated, and accused them of continuing to treat women as second-class citizens in every way.

Her book made a great impression on American journalist Betty Friedan, who touched off an explosion of her own with her book, *The Feminine Mystique*. Writing of the discontent women felt in leading unfulfilled lives dedicated to housework and child care, Friedan gave powerful voice to the frustrations many women were feeling in the '50s and '60s. Her book became the touchstone of the modern middle-class feminist revolution, which is still being fought today.

FOUR

At the urging of feminists, Friedan founded the National Organization for Women (NOW). One of its first victories was winning an executive order banning the award of government contracts to companies or institutions found guilty of sex discrimination. This marked the first granting of power to women to enforce their right to jobs on an equal basis with men.

A black woman, tailor's assistant Rosa Parks, sparked a whole new civil rights movement in 1955 when she was jailed for refusing to yield her seat and move to the "blacks only" back of a Montgomery, Alabama, bus. Subsequently, feminists often joined civil rights leaders in pressing for equal rights for both blacks and women.

Feminists campaigning for reform helped enact the Equal Pay Act of 1963, the Civil Rights Act of 1964, and the 1964 Credit Law making credit more available to women, and Title IX of the Education Omnibus Act of 1972 prohibiting sex discrimination in schools. They also reintroduced the ERA in 1972.

In the late 1960s, students and young people revolted against the Vietnam War, and against an "establishment" they saw as unjust. Young women in the movement grew indignant at being relegated to the roles of coffee makers and envelope lickers. During a 1968 student strike at Columbia University, they demanded an equal share in decision-making. Not taken seriously, they withdrew from the strike to form their own separate women's protest group.

Feminist demonstrations made the women's liberation movement a prime topic for TV talk shows, magazines, and newspapers. In 1968, 1 feminists picketed the Miss America Pageant in Atlantic City. Denouncing the "degrading, mindless, boob-girlie symbol," the demonstrators burned their bras in protest. They castigated the pageant for judging women by how their looks pleased men, rather than on their value as individuals.

Betty Friedan considered bra-burning an unfortunate tactic. She believed it distorted campaigns for sexual equality by giving opponents an opportunity for ridicule, as well as frightening conventional women away from the movement. But feminists continued to fight beauty pageants as a major symbol of the way the media and its advertisers portrayed women to their detriment.

In 1970, author Kate Millett published a best-selling book, *Sexual Politics.* It documented her accusation that male-dominated societies had put women down for centuries, and that women had been brainwashed into accepting an inferior status by parents, peers, and society. "The exploitation of women rests on everything," she wrote. "It's all through our culture."

In that year, feminists broke into the CBS stockholders' annual meeting, charging CBS and the media with distorting and belittling women's image in commercials and programming. One shouted, "CBS abuses women. . . . You tell us to be happy housewives. We don't want to be slaves of any kind. You use our bodies to sell products. We don't want to be put out on the market. . . .

A subsequent in-house CBS memorandum, revealed by *Variety,* acknowledged, "Television must show a new image of a woman as a doer, as an educated, serious-minded individual person. Not just a kitchen slave or a single swinger. Acceptance of advertising hostile to women's dignity denigrates and causes the existent ridicule. . . . One thing is certain: the movement is definite and it is not going to go away."

Feminists also invaded newspaper offices to demand an end to sexist reporting. In June, 1970, Ben Bradlee, editor of the *Washington Post,* ordered reporters to write about women achievers with the same respect shown to male achievers, and not to use words like "brunette" or "cute" to describe women. Bradlee also ordered that women be hired and promoted at the same rate as men.

In 1972, journalist Gloria Steinem founded *Ms.* magazine, which soon became the bible of the feminist movement. Controversial, its sexual frankness led upset parents to try to ban it from high school libraries. Some feminist leaders criticized *Ms.* for running sexist liquor and cigarette ads along with its articles on women's rights. Senior editor Mary Thom defended the ads as the price *Ms.* had to pay for achieving a circulation of half a million.

Significantly, in the year that *Ms.* appeared, feminists supported the campaign of a woman running for president—black ex-congresswoman Shirley Chisholm.

One of the greatest successes of the women's movement was its campaign to abolish anti-abortion laws. In 1973, the Supreme Court finally decided in *Roe* v. *Wade* that abortion should be a matter of choice for each individual woman. This decision, however, was still bitterly fought over and was amended sixteen years later in 1989. A newly conservative Supreme Court gave each state the right to legislate its own abortion laws.

In 1974, the US Merchant Marine became the first government service school to enroll women. Connecticut's Ella Grasso became the first woman elected governor. The Little League bowed to feminist pressure and admitted girls to teams; Bunny Taylor, eleven, pitched the first no-hit game by a girl in Clay, West Virginia.

During 1978 and 1979, feminists outraged by sexual assaults on women at night on streets and campuses mounted "Take Back the Night" marches in city after city, demanding better protection for women. To protect themselves, some women began carrying Mace in their handbags, while others attended martial arts classes to learn how to defend themselves against male attackers.

FIVE

Stirred by *Ms.* and the now-rapid growth of the feminist movement, more and more women resented the sexist portrayals of women in the male-dominated media. Local protest movements sprang up around the country. Typical was the movement led by a California model named Ann Simonton. Having modeled since she was fourteen, Simonton grew to resent the way advertisers and the media exploited models, using their bodies to sell products.

"It was dehumanizing, hurting my self-esteem," Simonton told me. "I felt very much like a prostitute because I was on display, at the whim of men to have me pose or act as they wanted."

Simonton had won several beauty contests, but also grew disillusioned with these. Their message to America, Simonton declared, was: "You have to have a beautiful face and figure to rate admiration. Plain, fat, and flat-chested women—get lost!"

Like feminists a generation earlier who had picketed the Miss America Pageant in Atlantic City, in 1982 Simonton led a protest demonstration against the Miss California Pageant in Santa Cruz. She created a sensation in a dress made of sewn-together bologna slices, with a neck ruff of hot dogs and a sprig of parsley. The costume symbolized her contention that the pageant was nothing more than a business-subsidized "meat market," capitalizing on women's bodies to promote commercial products. The media gave Simonton's crusade national coverage. Simonton also led feminist demonstrations against news dealers who sold lurid men's magazines featuring violent pornography. She charged that these encouraged sexual violence and rape. In contrast to the religious right's campaign for a legal ban on *all* portrayals of nudity and sex, which was a violation of the First Amendment, Simonton sought a voluntary withdrawal. Many store owners agreed with her, and removed the most violent men's magazines from their shelves.

When the Reagan administration took office in 1980, the women's movement feared that his ultra-conservative policies would thwart the struggle for equal rights. They put on drives and demonstrations to impress upon him their political power. To appease American women, in 1981 Reagan appointed Sandra Day O'Connor as the first woman justice of the US Supreme Court, and the Senate hastily confirmed her by a vote of 99–0.

The growing influence of the women's movement was not lost on the National Aeronautics and Space Administration, either. In 1983, Sally Ride made feminist history by being the first woman astronaut selected to shoot into space when the *Challenger* shuttle was launched from Cape Canaveral, Florida.

A year later, the Democratic party also acknowledged the strength of the women's movement by breaking tradition and nominating a woman, Geraldine Ferraro, as its vice-presidential candidate to run with presidential candidate Walter Mondale. She was the first woman to achieve this position in one of America's two major parties.

SIX

By the late 1980s, many women were achieving professional success on equal terms with their male colleagues. In 1988, the Supreme Court upheld a ban on sex discrimination in private clubs. Recognized as important sources of business connections, the all-male bastions of power were forced to open their doors to women members.

By 1989, more women were occupying key positions in television network news than ever before. The CBS Washington bureau was literally run by women, and half the network's US bureaus were headed by them. Both ABC and NBC also had women in many key positions. NBC disclosed that about 40 percent of the news division's management and professional positions were filled by women. Pamela Hill, vice president and executive producer for ABC News, said, "A lot has changed; it's a remarkable change."

In TV programming, the image of women that was presented to America also underwent improvements. Back in 1961, the program *Leave It to Beaver* had one character talking about the kind of girl a man should marry: "Oh, some very sensible girl from a nice family. One with both feet on the ground, who's a good cook and can keep a nice house and see that he's happy."

But TV sitcoms in 1989 featured different kinds of heroines. One was the overweight, funny, working mother Roseanne, who won her audiences by shouting, "I am woman. Hear me *roar!* Candice Bergen's character, the TV reporter Murphy Brown, was, in Bergen's words, "a real scrapper." Many TV dramas showed women as quite satisfied living without husbands or children and pursuing professional careers.

Even more surprising, men were also beginning to yearn for liberation from their own traditional lives. In the book *Quiet Desperation: The Truth About Successful Men,* Jan Halper wrote, "They were beginning to question their roles, re-evaluate their career goals and dreams, alter their lifestyles and redefine their personal relationships. They said they felt betrayed by the system to which they gave their hearts and souls. 'I don't want to play this game anymore,' was the message men were giving to me."

Over a dozen women writers and producers regularly lunched together as the "Class of '72." That was the year the Equal Employment Opportunity Act extended civil rights protections to private industry, opening the doors of TV networks and movie studios to women seeking key positions.

In 1989, Joyce Kennard, an Indonesian-born immigrant who spent her youth oppressed by poverty and racial segregation, became the second woman ever appointed to the California Supreme Court.

"We have seen enormous changes in the role of women in society during the past twenty years, changes we now take for granted," Betty Friedan recently declared. She also noted, "After all, any daughter can now dream of being an astronaut, after Sally Ride, or running for president, after Geraldine Ferraro."

These achievements and aspirations would not have been possible without the work of three women. In the stories of these three feminists, one can see the development of the women's revolution from its inception to its present-day status.

They were important catalysts in each phase of that revolution, changing the lives and destinies of women as never before. They made possible the modern woman of tomorrow, a woman who will be even more liberated when the dreams of Susan B. Anthony, Margaret Sanger, and Betty Friedan are wholly fulfilled.

Susan B. Anthony

1820–1906

"Give women an equal chance!"

ONE

Judge Ward Hunt, newly appointed Supreme Court justice for the state of New York, glowered down at the defiant woman dressed in black silk who had committed the crime of voting illegally in the 1872 elections. Then he read out his written opinion on the case, prepared even before he heard arguments by the defendant's lawyers.

"Gentlemen of the jury," he said sternly, "you will return with a verdict finding the defendant guilty as charged."

Susan B. Anthony's outraged lawyer leaped to his feet.

"Your Honor," he protested, "the Court has no power to make such a direction in a criminal case. We insist that the jury be permitted to bring in its *own* verdict!"

Judge Hunt ignored him. The all-male jury meekly obeyed his order: "Guilty as charged!" The next day, Hunt rejected a motion by the defense for a new trial, and ordered Susan to stand up.

"Has the prisoner anything to say why sentence shall not be pronounced?"

"Yes, Your Honor, I have many things to say," she replied. "For in your ordered verdict of guilty, you have trampled underfoot every vital principle of our government. . . . Robbed of the fundamental privilege of citizenship, I am degraded from the status of a citizen to that of a subject. And not only myself individually, but all of my sex are, by Your Honor's verdict, doomed to political subjection under this so-called republican form of government."

"The Court cannot listen," Judge Hunt fumed, "to a rehearsal of an argument which the prisoner's counsel has already consumed three hours in presenting."

"I am simply stating, Your Honor, the reasons why sentence cannot, in justice, be pronounced against me. Your denial of my citizen's right to vote is the denial of my right of consent as one of the governed; the denial of my right of representation as one of the taxed; the denial of my right to a trial by a jury of my peers as an offender against law; therefore, the denial of my sacred right to life, liberty, property, and—"

"The Court cannot allow the prisoner to go on!" roared the judge. The tall, angular woman with gray eyes and chestnut hair twisted into a bun refused to be intimidated.

"But Your Honor will not deny me this one and only poor privilege of protest against this high-handed outrage upon my citizen's rights," she persisted. "May it please the Court to remember that, since the day of my arrest last November, this is the first time that either myself or any person of my disenfranchised class has been allowed a word of defense. . . ."

"The prisoner must sit down!" Judge Hunt bellowed. "The Court cannot allow it!"

"Had Your Honor submitted my case to the jury, as was clearly your duty," Susan persisted, "even then I should have had just cause of protest, for not one of those men was my peer . . . each and every man of them was my political superior. . . . Precisely as no disfranchised person is entitled to sit upon a jury, and no woman is entitled to the franchise, so none but a regularly admitted lawyer is allowed to practice in the courts, and no woman can gain admission to the bar. Hence, jury, judge, counsel—all must be my superiors."

"The Court must insist that the prisoner has been tried according to the established forms of law!"

"Yes, Your Honor, but by forms of law all made by men, interpreted by men, administered by men, in favor of men and against women. Hence Your Honor's ordered verdict of guilty, against a United States citizen for the exercise of the 'citizen's right to vote,' simply because that citizen was a woman and not a man." Susan took a deep breath.

"Not long ago," she pointed out, "the same man-made law made it a crime punishable by a thousand-dollar fine and six months in prison to give a cup of cold water or a crust of bread to a panting [slave] fugitive tracking his way to Canada. Every man or woman in whose veins coursed a drop of human sympathy violated that wicked law, reckless of consequences and was justified in so doing. As then the slaves who got their freedom had to take it over or under or through the unjust forms of law, precisely so now must women take it to get their right to a voice in this government. And I have taken mine, and mean to take it at every opportunity!"

Apoplectic with rage, Judge Hunt howled, "The Court orders the prisoner to sit down! *It will not allow another word!*"

But Susan was still not finished. "When I was brought before Your Honor for trial, I hoped for a broad and liberal interpretation of the Constitution and its recent amendments, which should declare . . . equality of rights the national guarantee to all persons born or naturalized in the United States. But failing to get this justice . . ." she paused and raised her chin defiantly, ". . . I ask not leniency at your hands, but rather the full rigor of the law!"

The infuriated judge snarled, "The sentence of the Court is that you pay a fine of one hundred dollars and the costs of the prosecution."

Susan Anthony's chin went up even higher. "May it please Your Honor, I will *never* pay a dollar of your unjust penalty. . . . And I shall earnestly and persistently continue to urge all women to the practical recognition of the old Revolutionary maxim, *'Resistance to tyranny is obedience to God!'* "

Refusing to pay the fine, she challenged Judge Hunt to hold her in custody or send her to jail until it was paid. He did neither, aware that this would enable her to appeal her case directly to the US Supreme Court. He knew his arbitrary sentence would be overturned because a true trial by jury had been denied her.

By refusing Susan Anthony her chance to argue the right of woman suffrage before the US Supreme Court, Judge Hunt helped assure that women would not get the vote for another twenty-eight years.

TWO

Susan Anthony was born in South Adams, Massachusetts, on February 15, 1820. Her father, Daniel, was a liberal Quaker abolitionist who defied church frowns by marrying a Baptist, Susan's mother, Lucy. They had six children—four girls, Guelma, Susan, Hannah, and Mary—and two sons, Daniel, and J. Merritt.

Susan worshipped her father, an intelligent, enterprising storekeeper who also owned and managed small cotton mills. It was her father's refusal to purchase cotton raised by slave labor that first made Susan aware of the evils of slavery.

In 1826, the family moved to Battenville, New York. Daniel settled his growing family in a fifteen-room brick house. It included a store and a schoolroom where his own and his neighbors' children were taught by a hired teacher. She was not allowed to teach music because Quakers considered music and dancing immoral frivolities. Susan grew up never having danced or sung children's songs.

In the Quaker church women sat on one side, men on the other. Yet Susan never had any doubts about the equality of the sexes because the Quakers treated both equally. She grew up convinced that she was the equal of any man, and deserved to be recognized as such.

The Anthony children were usually dressed in simple, drab clothing as befitting modest, God-fearing Quaker youngsters.

Once, however, Susan's mother could not resist buying her a bright Scotch-plaid coat. Susan was thrilled and would admire herself in a mirror whenever she wore it. One day, a dog jumped up on her and ripped a huge hole in it. Anguished, Susan wondered whether this was God's way of punishing her for her vanity.

The most serious of the Anthony girls, Susan dutifully did more than her share of the bed making, dishwashing, cooking, and cleaning. As a young teenager, she became interested in the young women and girls who came to work in her father's mill for the prevailing wage of $1.50 a week and board in her father's big house. Daniel Anthony considered them part of his extended family and began an evening school for them. Joining his temperance society, they pledged never to drink hard liquor.

Once, when one of the mill workers was ill, fourteen-year-old Susan prevailed upon her father to let her substitute as a spooler. During the two weeks she worked there, she was taught and helped by Sally Ann Hyatt, a skilled weaver from Vermont who was the mill's best troubleshooter. When Susan's father appointed a male worker as mill supervisor, Susan was puzzled.

"Since Sally Ann knows much more about weaving and the machinery than he does," she asked, "why didn't you appoint her supervisor instead?"

Daniel Anthony shook his head. "Supervision of labor has always been for men, Susan. It would never do to have a woman overseer in the mill."

Susan was shocked. This was her first intimation that women faced discrimination in the working world. She soon became aware that women could become only teachers, nurses, farm help, factory workers, or maids, at wages always lower than men received for similar work. Women's pay ranged from $1.00 to $3.00 a week, out of which they often had to pay as much as $1.75 for board.

At fifteen, Susan taught in a district school for $1.50 and board. It was the beginning of a teaching career that lasted until she was thirty-two.

In 1836, when Susan was sixteen, her father sent her to Miss Deborah Moulson's Seminary for Females. Susan had a miserable time. Miss Moulson had taken a strong dislike to her and gave her failing grades. Once she tongue-lashed Susan for not knowing the rule for "dotting an 'i.'"

"This was like an Electrical shock to me," Susan wrote in her diary. "I rushed upstairs to my room where, without restraint, I could give vent to my tears. . . . I do consider myself such a bad creature that I cannot see any who seems worse."

Susan was rescued from Miss Moulson by her father's business failure, caused by the severe depression of 1837. Daniel Anthony's company went so deeply into debt that everything the family owned had to be sold at auction. Susan was upset when the sheriff seized her mother's dearest personal possessions. The law that allowed this seemed grossly unfair to wives.

Susan was also disturbed by the fact that women, blacks, and Indians were denied the right to vote. She resolved that one day she would work to reform all discriminatory male laws.

Her father moved the family into an abandoned tavern in Center Falls, New York, where he sought to recoup his fortune by logging, farming, and becoming the local postmaster.

At nineteen, Susan fell in love with a handsome young man named Aaron McLean. He did not, however, see eye to eye with her on the question of female equality. Aaron considered, for example, that Susan's advocacy of women to have the same right as men to become preachers was ridiculous.

In 1839, she was offered a teaching job at a Quaker school for girls in New Rochelle. Attending lectures in the city, she broadened her understanding of civic issues. She grew determined to do what she could to combat the evils of drink, slavery, prostitution, and sexist laws.

Enthusiastic about one woman lecturer, Susan wrote Aaron, "I guess if you could hear her you would believe in a woman's preaching. What an absurd notion that women have not intellectual and moral faculties sufficient for anything but domestic concerns!"

Apparently their different outlooks turned Aaron away from Susan. She was stunned when he chose as his bride not herself, but her sister Guelma. When she visited the newlyweds with some biscuits she had baked, she told them proudly that she had been studying algebra.

"I'd rather see a woman make biscuits like these," her new brother-in-law said, munching one, "than solve the knottiest problem in algebra."

"There is no reason," Susan replied icily, "why she should not be able to do both!"

Soon after Aaron's marriage, Susan was asked for her hand by a young man who also asked her to give up teaching. Since she did not care for him, and had no intention of substituting housework for teaching, she refused.

Several years later, she had another proposal from a well-to-do elderly Quaker. She sent him on his way, too, sighing, "These old bachelors are perfect nuisances to society." When one of Susan's friends married a man far less intelligent than she, Susan commented in her diary, " 'Tis passing strange that a girl possessed of common sense should be willing to marry a lunatic—but so it is."

She began to feel that one way or another she was not fated to become a wife. Nor was she sure that she cared too much. She confided to her diary, "I should think any female would rather live and die an old maid." Judging from what she saw around her, even in her own home, Susan viewed the life of a married woman as filled with hard work, sacrifice, and little joy, whereas husbands lived as kings.

In her growing animosity toward the male sex, Susan considered it ridiculous to idolize any man. When President Martin Van Buren visited New Rochelle, she wrote home, "Large crowds of people called to look at him as if he were a puppet show.

Really, one would have thought an angelic being had descended from heaven, to have heard and seen the commotion . . . merely to look at a human being who is possessed of nothing more than any ordinary man and therefore should not be worshipped more than any mortal being."

She also felt disturbed when the president set a "bad example" by attending the theater, and by having wine with his dinner, "enjoying this wickedness," while "many poor, dear children were crying for food and for water to allay their thirst."

THREE

Susan greatly admired the sisters Angelina and Sarah Grimké who, with Lucretia Mott, set up the Underground Railroad to help slaves escape from the South to the North. This was the beginning of the abolitionist movement, whose ranks Susan soon joined in her determination to help oppressed Americans.

Raised to dread the evils of drink, Susan was appalled by those who enjoyed spirits, even in moderation. Once, visiting her aunt and uncle, she became upset when her uncle took cider and ale with his dinner. She later wrote him deploring his fall into sin. He replied whimsically, "We should think from the shape of thy letter that thou thyself hadst had a good horn from the contents of the cider barrel, a part being written one side up and a part the other way."

Susan attended anti-slavery meetings held in her father's home. She listened avidly to descriptions of the Underground Railroad, and of the political controversy over slavery. When she attended a Quaker meeting in New Rochelle, she was shocked by a commotion the Friends made because a black man chose to attend. Some Friends stalked out of the meeting house indignantly.

"What a lack of Christianity is this!" Susan deplored.

She was also angered by another action taken by the Friends against her father. Young people in Center Falls had persuaded Daniel Anthony to let them hold a dance on the third floor of his tavern home. He agreed reluctantly, because otherwise they would have had to hold it in the town tavern's ballroom, where they would be exposed to alcohol.

Outraged, the anti-dancing Friends of Center Falls read Susan's father out of the Society. Displaying a stubborn streak Susan was also soon to manifest, he persisted in attending meetings, even though he could have no voice in them.

In 1845, hard times forced the Anthonys to move again, this time to a farm in Rochester. The next year, Susan was offered a job as head women's teacher at the Canajoharie Academy. Living at the home of her easygoing uncle, Joshua Reed, for three years, she found the stern teachings of her Quaker upbringing starting to erode. Influenced by her two lighthearted girl cousins, Susan discarded both her Quaker dress and speech.

Out of bright materials she bought, she made herself pretty dresses, which she wore with lace mitts and flower-trimmed bonnets. One visitor to her classroom commented, "The schoolmarm looks beautiful!"

At twenty-five, Susan learned to dance, enjoying it immensely. But going to a dance with one attractive man, she found her evening spoiled by his unsteadiness on the dance floor.

"I certainly shall not attend another dance," she wrote her sister Mary, "unless I have a total abstainer to accompany me!"

Crusades against drinking were becoming increasingly widespread because of the number of workers who drank away their wages, leaving their families destitute. The leading anti-liquor organization was the Sons of Temperance. Women seeking to join were rejected, told disdainfully, "Let you women keep your silence!" Angrily, they organized themselves instead as the Daughters of Temperance.

Susan joined the chapter in Canajoharie, and in 1848 formed a new chapter in Albany. Appointed to chair a fair and supper to raise funds, she made her first public speech.

"In my humble opinion," Susan declared, "all that is needed to produce a complete Temperance and Social Reform . . . is for our Sex to cast their United influences into the balance." Her intense, earnest speech won resounding applause, casting twenty-eight-year-old Susan into the spotlight as a bright young woman who dared defy the male credo that women were to be seen but not heard.

FOUR

On July 19, 1848, Elizabeth Cady Stanton and Lucretia Mott organized their Women's Rights Convention in Seneca Falls, New York. Three hundred women and men met to sign a Declaration of Independence for Women. They demanded not only woman suffrage, but also justice for the American wife, because "man has made her, if married, civilly dead." Wives, they insisted, should have full equality with their husbands before the law in all respects.

Publicized as a news oddity, the convention excited nationwide interest. From 1848 until the Civil War in 1861, Women's Rights Conventions were held nearly every year in different cities in the East and Midwest. Those who attended were largely from educated, native-born, Protestant, middle-class families that acknowledged the need to reform social evils.

Increasingly, the right to speak at these conventions was restricted to women only. And as the movement gained strength, it drew ever harsher and angrier attacks from male-dominated churches, government offices, and newspapers.

When Susan returned home on vacation in August, she found that her father, mother, and sister Mary had attended a continuation of the Women's Rights Convention in Rochester, and had signed the Declaration. Giving Susan enthusiastic reports about Mrs. Stanton and Mrs. Mott, they urged her to join the movement.

But Susan felt that her temperance crusade was more important. Besides, wasn't the law beginning to recognize women's rights? In 1848, the New York Legislature had passed the Married Women's Property Law, permitting a wife to keep her own inherited property.

Susan decided not to return to her teaching job in Canajoharie because the new principal was an unpleasant Southerner who was the son of a slaveholder. She was also irked by the discovery that male teachers were being paid four times as much as she was. Studying the situation of women workers in the United States, Susan found that almost one out of four factory employees were women who needed to work, invariably for less pay than men.

She was also bothered that wives worked hard at home caring for their families, often with little recognition or reward.

"Woman," Susan decided, "has been the great unpaid laborer of the world." As though to prove her point, she performed hard physical work on the family farm picking peaches, preserving them, helping with the housework, and weaving carpets.

While not relinquishing her temperance work, Susan became inspired by her father's enthusiasm for abolition. Every Sunday, she helped her mother prepare dinner for abolitionists who gathered at their home. She listened eagerly to such famous guests as Frederick Douglass, William Lloyd Garrison, and Wendell Phillips.

Fierce public opposition in the North to the antislavery movement did not dissuade Susan from taking part in it. She joined a wife and husband abolitionist team on tour for a week, admiring their courage as they addressed mobs that threw rotten eggs at them and threatened violence. When the Society of Friends in Rochester rejected abolition, Susan and her father gave up being Quakers and joined the liberal Unitarians.

FIVE

In May, 1851, Susan travelled to Seneca Falls to hear Garrison speak. She stayed with Mrs. Amelia Bloomer, editor of a new temperance magazine, *The Lily*, which had created a sensation by advocating the new "bloomer" costume for women.

Susan was thrilled when Mrs. Bloomer introduced her to the now-famous Elizabeth Cady Stanton. Elizabeth, in turn, was greatly impressed with the younger Susan. The two quickly formed a friendship that lasted a lifetime as they fought side by side in reformist crusades. Elizabeth did most of the thinking, writing, and speaking. Susan did most of the organizing.

They made a contrasting pair on speaking platforms—Susan tall, intense, anxious, reserved, quiet, and dignified; Elizabeth barely five feet tall, plump, cheerful, brilliant, witty, and impetuous. Susan, who was five years younger, had great respect for Elizabeth. She addressed Elizabeth as "Mrs. Stanton," while Elizabeth called her Susan.

Frequently Susan had to carry on alone because Elizabeth had to drop her work with the movement to care for her husband and seven children. When Susan was scheduled to speak to a teachers' convention, she begged Elizabeth to put aside her home duties long enough to write a speech for her to deliver. She knew that if Elizabeth wrote it, it would be brilliant.

The Rochester Daughters of Temperance sent Susan as a delegate to the 1851 state convention of the Sons of Temperance. When she rose to propose a resolution, the indignant male chairman snapped, "The sisters were not invited here to speak, but to listen and learn!" Outraged, Susan and the other women delegates stormed out of the hall.

Guided by Elizabeth's advice, Susan founded their own New York state temperance organization. Their first convention in 1851 was a great success. Elizabeth was elected president, and

ONE OF THE DELIGHTFUL RESULTS OF BLOOMERISM.—THE LADIES WILL
POP THE QUESTION.

Superior Creature. "SAY! OH, SAY, DEAREST! WILL YOU BE MINE?" &C., &C.

A cartoon from *Punch*, deriding *Mrs. Bloomer's fashion*, about 1850.

The women's rights movement was frequently the object of ridicule in the press. *Above*, a cartoon from an 1850s issue of *Punch* satirizes Mrs. Bloomer's fashion. *Below*, a 1909 cartoon derides the suffragettes for shunting child care onto their husbands.

Susan secretary, of the new Woman's State Temperance Society (WSTS), which quickly gained 20,000 members.

Susan and Elizabeth dared speak at the 1851 convention in the new bloomer costume, sparking one paper's sneer that Susan "resembled a man." As the controversy over women's wearing the bloomer costume raged, Elizabeth argued that it would let women enter more male occupations, in which hoopskirts would hamper them. Many conventional women were shocked by it, however, regarding it as an immoral display of female legs. Men considered it a ridiculous attempt by feminists to "wear the pants" in marriage.

"If women mean to wear the pants," editor James Gordon Bennett wrote mockingly in his *New York Herald*, "then they must also be ready in case of war to buckle on the sword!"

To their dismay, Susan, Elizabeth, and the other feminists found the public far more agitated by their "reform dress" than by their ideas for social reform. Most feminists who dared to wear bloomers grew increasingly exasperated by the howling, egg-throwing mobs who followed them in the streets. Wherever they went, men whistled and made suggestive remarks, while small boys chanted crude street songs of derision.

Susan received such ridicule wearing the bloomers that Elizabeth advised her to stop wearing and defending the costume. "It is not wise, Susan," she wrote, "to use so much energy and feeling that way. You can put them to better use."

Susan and Elizabeth, as well as other feminists and even Mrs. Bloomer herself, eventually felt compelled to abandon dress reform. Susan threw all her energies into crusading for temperance, abolition, and women's rights. She sought to speed the day when women would "have independent incomes," and would be paid for their work "with wages as men are."

More and more, she grew to realize that the only way she could hope to achieve her objectives was first to win the vote for women. Without the right to elect representatives pledged to promote their own causes, women would only be able to plead for justice instead of to enforce it.

SIX

By the time of the next Women's Rights Convention, held at Syracuse, New York, on September 8, 1852, the feminists were stirring vigorous controversy in the press and in the pulpits. Lucretia Mott was elected president, and Susan secretary. Women reported on their efforts to spread the feminist doctrine, and to gather petitions for legislation to allow women to keep their own wages, wives to own property in their own names, and widows to be named guardians of their own children.

Syracuse churchmen denounced the women as "infidels" rebelling against the subordinate place allotted to them in the Bible. Editor Bennett asked in the *Herald:*

> How did woman first become subject to man, as she now is all over the world? By her nature, her sex, just as the negro is and always will be to the end of time, inferior to the white race and, therefore, doomed to subjection. . . . What do the leaders of the woman's rights convention want? They want to vote and to hustle with the rowdies at the polls. . . . They want to fill all other posts which men are ambitious to occupy, to be lawyers, doctors, captains of vessels, and generals in the field.

Bennett visualized a woman lawyer trying a case, and suddenly giving "birth to a fine bouncing boy in court!"

At the 1853 convention of the Women's State Temperance Society, Susan and Elizabeth were severely criticized for devoting too much talk to women's rights. Why didn't they confine themselves to promoting the temperance crusade? In a defiant reply, Elizabeth declared that any woman married to a habitual drunkard ought to have the legal right to divorce him.

In the uproar that followed, the delegates voted to allow men to become officers of the WSTS, and to speak. Men present promptly denounced Elizabeth for refusing to rely on prayer to solve women's problems. Susan indignantly sprang to Elizabeth's defense in a furious speech. When the convention voted Elizabeth out as president, Susan angrily resigned as secretary.

"Waste no more powder on the Women's State Temperance Society," Elizabeth told Susan. "We have other and bigger fish to fry!" Both took leave of the organization that they had founded.

———————

At thirty-three, Susan more and more took on the appearance of a fanatical crusader. Her tight, downward-curving lips, a new severe hairstyle, her stern gaze and ringing voice marked her as a woman rebel utterly determined to force men to recognize women's equality.

Part of her appeal was the novelty of a woman speaking in public like a man to challenge prevailing mores, especially relations between the sexes. Her controversial views delighted many women and a scattering of liberal men. But many others came to boo, hiss, and catcall. Susan was outraged by mob attacks on some feminist speakers, but was never deterred from speaking out by danger to herself.

In August, 1853, she attended the State Teachers' Convention in Rochester. Two-thirds of the five hundred teachers attending were women, but in two days Susan did not hear a single woman speak. Not only were they ignored, but they were denied a vote.

"My heart was filled with grief and indignation," she wrote, "thus to see the minority, simply because they were men, presuming that in them was vested all wisdom and knowledge."

Susan set off a bombshell at the close of the second day by rising and demanding to speak. A half-hour debate ensued as to whether she should have that right. At last, reluctantly allowed, Susan challenged the male teachers: "Do you not see that so long as society says woman has not brains enough to be a doctor, lawyer, or minister, but has plenty to be a teacher, every man of you who condescends to teach, tacitly admits . . . that he has no more brains than a woman?"

Everyone at the convention gasped. Susan sat down. Later, as the women delegates left, many shrank from the defiant "fanatic."

Susan found that many local women's groups disbanded soon after being organized for lack of money. She blamed this on the fact that in most states it was illegal for wives to keep money they themselves earned.

In the winter of 1854, Susan braved snowstorms and bitter cold in upstate New York to collect signatures on a petition in a house-to-house campaign. Though the state legislature refused to answer the petition's plea to change the system whereby a wife's wages could be collected only by her husband, and whereby only fathers were given legal control over children, the 6,000 signatures Susan collected were a sign of her ability to rally public support.

No hardship deterred Susan in her determination to spread the female revolution. She held and spoke at meetings every other night as she travelled from town to town. While maintaining this exhausting pace, she frequently had to endure miserable food and freezing hotel rooms, so cold that in the morning she had to break the ice in the pitcher to take a cold sponge bath.

Even at this point, Susan did not lack for suitors. One wealthy Quaker put a horse sleigh at her disposal, and urged her to give up the hard life of a reformer to enjoy creature comforts as his wife. But by then, Susan was utterly devoted to leading the female crusade to free both women and the slaves.

"No true woman," she wrote, "could sacrifice herself for love of one man, and wind her life around his whims, instead of developing her own life and talents."

Asked years later whether she had ever been in love, Susan laughed. "A thousand times!" she replied. ". . . But I never loved anyone so much that I thought it would last. In fact, I never felt I could give up my life of freedom to become a man's housekeeper. When I was young, if a girl married poverty, she became a drudge. If she married wealth, she became a doll. Had I married at twenty-one, I would have been either a drudge or a doll for fifty-five years. Think of it!" And she laughed again.

Susan's relentless crusades absorbed every ounce of her energy. She became privately critical of Elizabeth for letting her family come first. And she was chagrined a year later when two dynamic woman reformers, Lucy Stone and Antoinette Brown, married. She had counted on them to campaign with her, but now grew resigned to carrying on alone.

"There is not one woman left who may be relied on," she moaned to Lucretia Mott. "All have first to please their husbands, after which there is little time or energy left to spend in any other direction."

SEVEN

In March, 1855, Susan joined Ernestine Rose, a feminist free-thinker, in a lecture tour of the slave border cities. This tour marked the beginning of Susan's fifty-year career as a travelling organizer for blacks' as well as women's rights.

"I have had Pro-Slavery People tell me just go South once," she wrote in her diary in Baltimore, "and see Slavery as it is, and then you will talk very differently. I can assure all such, that contact with Slavery has not a tendency to make me hate it less."

Worn out and ill from the hardships of incessant travel, Susan was forced to retreat to a sanitorium to take a "water cure." Fully recovered by the beginning of 1856, she returned to touring New York State with another lecturer, Frances D. Gage.

One night, they stopped at a small tavern. The owner's young wife cooked them dinner, washed the dishes, rocked her infant to sleep, ironed, prepared their room, then made their breakfast.

"When we came to pay our bill," Susan wrote home, "the dolt of a husband took the money and put it in his pocket. He had not lifted a hand to lighten that woman's burdens, but had sat and talked with the men in the bar room . . . yet the law gives him the right to every dollar she earns."

After two years of hard work collecting signatures on petitions for women's rights, Susan presented the petitions to the New York Legislature in March, 1856. They were received with snickers of derision. The Legislature's report mocked, "If there is any inequality or oppression in the case, the gentlemen are the sufferers."

Susan refused to be discouraged. That same year some of the legislative reforms she had sought in the 1852 Women's Rights Convention were granted by the states of Ohio and Nebraska in response to feminist campaigns there.

By this time, Susan had developed into a spellbinding speaker whose reputation attracted large audiences. Asked to become an agent of the American Anti-Slavery Society (AASS), she was put in charge of the abolitionist party in New York State.

If she had met with indifference or ridicule from many who heard her speak on women's rights, now she faced dangerous hostility in her new crusade. Only five years from the outbreak of the Civil War, slavery was a fiercely debated and controversial issue. Most Northerners regarded abolitionists as hot-headed fanatics. Susan and other speakers were pelted with rotten eggs, booed, jeered, drowned out with catcalls and bawdy songs.

Addressing a teachers' convention, Susan called for equal schooling for black children, as well as coeducation, extremely radical ideas for their time. Elizabeth Stanton's husband Henry told his wife, *"You* stir up Susan, and *she* stirs up the world!"

At women's rights conventions, Susan and Elizabeth continued to demand more liberal divorce laws to end women's subservient status in marriage. The press denounced them scathingly.

At one meeting, an anti-slavery clergyman rebuked Susan, saying, "You are not married. You have no business to be discussing marriage!" Susan replied coolly, "Well, you are not a slave. Suppose you quit lecturing on slavery!"

When the government prepared to execute abolitionist John Brown for his raid on the US arsenal at Harper's Ferry and for the death of the town's mayor, Susan called a protest meeting in Rochester. Praising Brown's attempt to establish an independent republic for fugitive slaves, she mourned, "Not one man of prominence in religion or politics will publicly identify himself with the John Brown meeting."

In March, 1860, despite the derision Susan's effort had received four years earlier, she and Elizabeth worked on a new speech to be delivered before a joint session of the New York Legislature. This time when Elizabeth made their demands for equal rights for wives, to their surprise and gratification the chamber rang with enthusiastic applause.

The next day, the Assembly passed the Married Women's Property Bill, giving wives the right to their own wages, the right to own property in their own names, the right to an equal say with their husbands about their children, and the right to sue in court.

But Susan's jubilation at this victory was short-lived. Two years later, while she and other feminists were engrossed in the abolitionist movement, the New York Legislature quietly amended the 1860 act. Wives' equal guardianship over their children was cancelled, and control of the property of their minor children was taken away from widows.

"We deserve to suffer," Susan sighed to Lucretia Mott, "for our confidence in man's sense of justice."

That December, a woman separated from a brutal husband appealed to Susan personally to hide her and her thirteen-year-old daughter from him. Susan took them to New York City for shelter. When this became known to the woman's brothers, they threatened to have Susan arrested. Abolitionist leaders William Lloyd Garrison and Wendell Phillips urged Susan to return the woman and daughter to the husband. She flatly refused.

"Had I turned my back upon her," Susan told them, "I should have scorned myself. . . . I remembered only that I was a human being. . . . Trust me that as I ignore all law to help the slave, so will I ignore it all to protect an enslaved woman."

Her father wrote her, "Legally you are wrong, but morally you are right, and I will stand by you."

At the tenth national Women's Rights Convention, Elizabeth upset many delegates by delivering a powerful speech demanding a liberal divorce bill. When Wendell Phillips spoke against considering it, Susan rose to declare, "Marriage has ever been a one-sided matter, resting most unequally upon the sexes. . . . Down to the present day, woman has never been thought of other than as a piece of property, to be disposed of at the will and pleasure of man. . . . She must accept marriage as man proffers it or not at all." Marriage, Susan charged, was "involuntary servitude" for women, forbidden by the Thirteenth Amendment.

But the delegates refused to consider the divorce proposal.

The Civil War interrupted Susan's crusade for women's rights. Most Northern feminists voted to throw all their energies instead into patriotic support of the war effort. Susan spent a whole year working for and with fugitive slaves. In 1861, she noted in her diary that she had "outfitted a slave for Canada with the help of Harriet Tubman."

Susan held an anti-slavery rally in January at Buffalo. When she upbraided President Lincoln and the Northern states for failing to end segregation and laws prejudicial to blacks, she was howled down. The enraged mob hissed, hooted, yelled, and stamped their feet. They were joined in their vehement opposition by the police present, and Susan was forced to end the rally.

Mobs broke up her rallies in city after city. In Utica, when a drunken crowd gathered, the mayor begged Susan not to go ahead with her rally. He offered instead to escort her to a place of safety. "I am not afraid," she replied disdainfully. "It is you who are the coward. If you have the power to protect me in person, you have also the power to protect me in the right of free speech. I scorn your assistance!"

Denounced by Republican papers as a "pestiferous fanatic and infidel," Susan was pelted with rotten eggs in Syracuse, then forced to flee for her life as she was burned in effigy. But threats, insults, missiles, ridicule, and exhaustion failed to shake Susan's determination.

When Lincoln issued the Emancipation Proclamation in January, 1863, Susan was angered because it freed only Southern slaves as a war expedient. She and Elizabeth organized a Women's National Loyal League to demand full citizens' rights for both Northern slaves and all women. They collected 400,000 signatures on this petition. It helped influence Congress to pass the Thirteenth Amendment which abolished slavery, though it made no mention of women's rights.

Susan and Elizabeth supported male abolitionists' demands for the passage of a Fourteenth Amendment assuring full citizens' rights to the newly freed slaves. But Susan was shocked and enraged when they insisted on using the word "male" to describe intended beneficiaries of these rights. Elizabeth argued, "Put the word male in the Constitution, and it will take fifty years to get it out." But the male abolitionists insisted that this was no time to start a row over women's rights.

When the Fifteenth Amendment prohibiting the denial of voting rights because of race was debated, Susan fought in vain to add the words "or sex." She tongue-lashed the male abolitionists, declaring, "I would sooner cut off my right hand than ask for the ballot for the black man and not for woman." From that time on, she and Elizabeth crusaded for woman suffrage only, turning their first petition for it over to Congress in January, 1865.

"Up to this hour," Susan declared, "we have looked to State action only for the recognition of our rights. But now, by the results of the war, the whole question of suffrage reverts back to Congress and the US Constitution."

The next year they reorganized the women's rights movement to combine their demands for black and female voting rights.

The lines are drawn in the battle for women's suffrage. *Above*, women in Columbus, Ohio, gather in front of the Woman's Suffrage headquarters. *Below*, men are drawn to the headquarters of the National Association Opposed to Woman Suffrage.

Their new American Equal Rights Association (AERA) criticized the Fourteenth Amendment as "utterly inadequate" from women's point of view. But opponents of the woman's vote argued that it would somehow destroy family life, the church, and the government. The vote for women was still over half a century away.

Susan turned her efforts toward getting woman suffrage adopted by a New York state constitutional convention. She sought the support of Horace Greeley, abolitionist publisher of the powerful New York *Tribune*.

"No!" he snapped. "You must not get up any agitation for that measure. . . . Help us get the word 'white' out of the Constitution. This is the Negro's hour. . . . Your turn will come next."

But Susan pressed her demand at the convention.

"If you vote," Greeley sneered, "are you ready to fight?"

"Yes, Mr. Greeley," Susan snapped back, "just as you fought in the late war—-at the point of a goose quill!"

She reminded the delegates that hundreds of women, disguised as men, had fought in the Civil War. When Greeley insisted that "the women of our state do not choose to vote," Susan sprang a humiliating surprise. She produced a petition asking for the vote signed by three hundred Westchester women, and included among them was Greeley's own wife!

EIGHT

On a speaking tour in Kansas, Susan and Elizabeth met George Francis Train, a handsome, wealthy Democratic eccentric. He offered to back Susan's dream of a weekly newspaper to promote women's rights, and gave it a name—*The Revolution*. The first issue appeared in January, 1868. Its masthead motto read: "The true republic—men, their rights and nothing more; women, their rights and nothing less."

In addition to urging woman suffrage, *The Revolution* questioned unfairness in the institutions of marriage, law, and organized religion. It argued against different moral standards for men and women. More eyebrows were raised by its call for justice for blacks, workers, and prostitutes.

"While we would not refuse man an occasional word in our columns," one editorial declared, "yet as masculine ideas have ruled the race for six thousand years, we especially desire that *The Revolution* shall be the mouthpiece for women."

To Susan's dismay, after just the first issue, Train left for England to help the Irish rebels, only to be arrested and imprisoned. Susan noted in her diary, "This is but another discipline to teach us that we must stand on our own feet." For three years she struggled to raise the funds needed to keep *The Revolution* alive.

Organizing the Working Women's Association, Susan created a stir at the National Labor Union Convention when she sought a seat as the WWA's delegate. Labor leaders agreed to seat her only after making it clear that they would not endorse her "peculiar ideas." But Susan pursued her fight against the low wages, long hours, and unhealthy factory conditions suffered by women forced into the workplace.

The Revolution carried news of all working women's associations being formed, and served as their inspiration to strike against exploitive employers. She united the groups into one new Workingwomen's Central Association (WCA). Elected its president, Susan encouraged women typesetters in Albany to form their own union, the first of its kind in the country.

"Join the Union, girls," Susan urged in *The Revolution,* "and together say *Equal Pay for Equal Work!*"

Upset employers threatened to fire unionized women workers. Worried husbands and fathers warned working women not to have anything to do with that troublemaker, Susan Anthony.

In 1868, Susan championed the cause of Hester Vaughn in the pages of *The Revolution*. Hester was a Welsh girl who had been raped by her employer, then cast out of her home destitute and pregnant. Her child, born in a freezing garret, had died. At a Pennsylvania trial, she was not permitted to speak in her own defense because she was a woman. Found guilty of murdering her infant by an all-male jury, she was sentenced to be hanged.

Susan and Elizabeth organized a mass meeting of women to protest. They demanded that women should be tried before a jury of their peers—other women. And why were women still denied a vote in making the laws, or prevented from voting for the officials who executed those laws? The rally also went on record as opposing the death penalty as barbarous.

The governor of Pennsylvania was urged by Susan, Elizabeth, and their followers to pardon Hester Vaughn as a victim of injustice. He agreed that women could never receive true justice until women were allowed on juries, and pardoned Hester. She was allowed to return to her native Wales.

On March 15, 1869, Susan and Elizabeth got Congressman George W. Julian of Indiana to offer a constitutional amendment providing the right to vote without discrimination because of sex. This was the first federal woman suffrage amendment ever proposed in Congress. Congressmen turned a deaf ear.

To pressure them, Susan and Elizabeth held a series of conventions around the country. One Milwaukee paper described Susan as "an earnest, enthusiastic, fiery woman—ready, apt, witty and what a politician would call sharp . . . radical in the strongest sense." The *Hartford Post* noted, "Miss Anthony is a resolute, substantial woman of forty or fifty, exhibiting no signs of age or weariness. Her hair is dark, her head well formed, her face has an expression of masculine strength. If she were a man you would guess that she was a schoolmaster, or a quiet clergyman, or perhaps a businessman and deacon. She pays no special attention to feminine graces, but is not ungraceful or unwomanly."

The American Equal Rights Association (AERA) that Susan and Elizabeth had founded three years earlier had now fallen under the control of male abolitionists. When the new male leaders insisted that the AERA had to concentrate on blacks' right to vote, not on the ballot for women, Susan and Elizabeth indignantly led a walkout.

They founded a new organization, the National Woman Suffrage Association (NWSA). Opposing the Fifteenth Amendment because it was limited to blacks, they offered instead a new Sixteenth Amendment that would guarantee the vote for all citizens. Once this passed, they planned to address controversial issues such as women's rights in marriage, and to challenge church credos about women's place in society.

Lucy Stone disagreed with these auxiliary goals, arguing that a woman's suffrage association, to be accepted as "respectable," had to limit itself to that issue alone. Accordingly, she organized a rival organization, the American Woman Suffrage Association (AWSA). Male reformers served as editors of a moderate AWSA paper, *The Woman's Journal.* A year later, its success put the more radical *The Revolution* out of business. Susan was saddled with a $10,000 debt. Advised to escape it by declaring bankruptcy, she replied, "My pride for women, to say nothing of my conscience, says no."

To press home to Congress the demands of the NWSA, Susan organized its 1870 convention in the nation's capital. At her appeal, Elizabeth interrupted a lecture tour in St. Louis to attend. "Of course, I stand by you to the end," she told Susan. "I would not see you crushed by rivals even if to prevent it required my being cut into inch bits."

The convention celebrated women's suffrage victories in England's municipal elections, and cheered the territories of Wyoming and Utah for enfranchising women.

There was now national recognition that Susan's tireless twenty years of campaigning was largely responsible for the tide's slowly beginning to turn for women. New York admirers held a celebration in honor of her fiftieth birthday. Many newspapers which had often crucified and ridiculed her now paid grudging respects.

The *New York World* called her "the Moses of her sex." The *Sun* called her "A Brave Old Maid." Even her mortal foe, Horace

Greeley, admitted in his *Tribune*, "Through these years of dispu-
tation and struggling, Miss Anthony has thoroughly impressed
friends and enemies alike with the sincerity and earnestness of
her purpose. . . ."

On the other hand, when she sought to attend the National
Labor Congress in Philadelphia to demand the admission of
women to all labor unions, she was barred. The *Utica Herald*
scoffed, "Who does not feel sympathy for Susan Anthony?
She has striven long and earnestly to become a man. . . . She
has never done any good in the world, but then she doesn't
think so."

NINE

During one of her constant lecture tours Susan met a district
judge who complained that his son, sent to law school, only
wanted to paint in a garret somewhere, while his daughter had
a splendid legal mind. "What a pity," the judge sighed, "that she
was not born a boy!"

Susan told a lecture audience angrily, "Only think—a brain
wasted because it happens to be a woman's. For this reason one
half the brains in the world remain undeveloped. How will we
remedy this? Give woman an equal chance to compete with men,
educate her and surround her with the same legal advantages."

Susan and Elizabeth were bemused by the sudden emergence
into political prominence of a beautiful and notorious adven-
turess named Victoria Woodhull. In January, 1871, through
one of her lovers in the Senate, she succeeded in winning an
appearance before a congressional committee to argue that
the Fourteenth and Fifteenth Amendments had already given
women the vote.

These amendments, she pointed out, declared all persons
born or naturalized in the US to be citizens, and all citizens to be
protected by the Constitution in their rights. Since all women

were "persons," and since suffrage was a right of citizenship, then they were entitled to vote!

Victoria's argument was promptly adopted by the NWSA, which advised its woman members to go to the polls and insist upon voting in the next election. The NWSA welcomed Victoria into its inner circle. She immediately sought to turn the NWSA into a political party. Elizabeth consented, but Susan was appalled, suspecting Victoria of secret ulterior motives.

"I was never so hurt with folly of Stanton," Susan wrote in her diary. She was proved correct when Victoria placed her own name in nomination for president of the United States.

The NWSA was further dismayed when Victoria was found to have had a dubious and immoral past. Admitting that she practiced "free love," Victoria scoffed at marriage as "legal prostitution." Elizabeth stood by her, but Susan distanced herself, worried that Victoria was bringing the whole woman suffrage movement into disrepute. Victoria, who published a scandal sheet, was arrested in 1872 for sending "obscene matter" through the mails because her newspaper carried a frank exposé of a famous minister's affair with a married woman. She conducted her presidential campaign from jail, largely through the intrigued press.

Meanwhile Susan spent six months making 108 lectures on an 8,000-mile tour of the West. She urged women to go to the polls and vote under the Fifteenth Amendment, daring election officials to rebuff them. To set the example herself, she returned to Rochester and assembled a group of women to vote with her in the presidential election of November, 1872.

To Susan's surprise, poll officials were too perplexed to stop them. But two weeks later, she was arrested for "illegal voting." Susan was delighted by the chance to challenge the government directly. Awaiting trial, she delivered stirring speeches in every district of the county on the subject: "Is it a crime for a US citizen to vote?"

"It is downright mockery to talk to women of their enjoyment of the blessings of liberty," she pointed out, "while they are denied the only means of securing them—the ballot." If everything in the Constitution and laws pertained only to men, Susan argued, then only men and not women should be subject to taxation and indictment under the criminal laws. She insisted that the Amendments made it clear that anything favoring human rights was constitutional, while anything against them was not.

"It is on this line," she vowed, "that we propose to fight our battle for the ballot—peaceably but nevertheless persistently—until we achieve complete triumph, and all United States citizens, men and women alike, are recognized as equals in the government."

Susan aroused so much indignation on her behalf in the county that the district attorney felt compelled to transfer the trial to another county to ensure a convicting jury.

After she was tried and found guilty in Judge Hunt's courtroom, three election inspectors who had permitted her to vote were also put on trial. Called as a witness, Susan was asked, "You presented yourself as a female, claiming you had a right to vote?" She replied, "I presented myself not as a female, sir, but as a citizen of the United States. I was called to the ballot box by the Fourteenth Amendment."

The inspectors were also found guilty, and fined by Judge Hunt. Two refused to pay their fines and were jailed. Susan appealed to a senator, who persuaded Ulysses S. Grant to pardon them.

The press was divided in its comments about Susan's conviction. Some papers denounced her as a shrew out to corrupt the law. Others praised her courage, dedication, ability, and the justice of her cause. The *Utica Observer* declared, "Such a case never before occurred in the history of our courts, and the hope is very general that it never will again. . . . Justice Hunt outraged the rights of Susan B. Anthony."

The *Worcester Spy* observed, "Miss Susan B. Anthony, whatever else she may be, is evidently of the right stuff for a reformer. . . .

She has argued her cause so well that almost all the male population of the county has been converted to her views." The *New York Daily Graphic* filled its front page with a full-length drawing of Susan wearing an Uncle Sam hat and a determined expression, over the caption "The Woman Who Dared."

As for Susan herself, she described the trials held by Judge Hunt as "the greatest judicial outrage history ever recorded! . . . A mere farce."

TEN

In 1873, Susan was criticized for having been involved with the controversial Victoria Woodhull. She replied angrily, "Cautious, careful people always casting about to preserve their reputation or social standards can never bring about reform. Those who are really in earnest are willing to be anything or nothing in the world's estimation, and . . . avow their sympathies with despised ideas and their advocates, and bear the consequences."

By strenuous, exhausting lecture tours, Susan was finally able to earn enough money to pay off the $10,000 in debts she owed when *The Revolution* failed. The press noted that by doing so Susan had behaved more honorably and responsibly than most businessmen, who would have either escaped into bankruptcy proceedings or paid off twenty cents on the dollar.

Susan constantly rushed to any state whose women appealed for her support on pending suffrage legislation. Often she spoke at meetings without fees. Her fame was such that President Grant permitted her to ask him in person, "Well, Mr. President, what are you going to do for woman suffrage?" He replied that he had done more for women than any other president by letting 5,000 women become postmasters.

By 1874, women's resentment of saloons had grown so great that a powerful new organization had been formed to combat drinking—the Women's Christian Temperance Union (WCTU).

Susan helped organize a branch in Rochester, but told its members, "The best thing this organization will do for you will be to show you how utterly powerless you are to put down the liquor traffic. . . . You will never be able to lessen this evil until you have votes."

While both major suffrage groups were active, the rival AWSA worked only to get the vote state by state, while Susan's organization, the NWSA, also pushed for a suffrage amendment to the federal Constitution. Susan's hopes were dealt a blow in 1875 when the US Supreme Court, while acknowledging that "women are persons and citizens," ruled that "the national Constitution does not confer the right of suffrage upon anyone." That right, said the Court, was up to states to determine.

In her lecture tour from state to state, Susan had to take trains at all hours of the night, occasionally even riding in freight cars. Often she was the only woman in a stagecoach filled with men. Enduring mud, snow, and prairie winds, she frequently had to appear on a lecture platform without having had anything to eat, or without time to bathe or change her dress. Her hotel rooms were often unheated and dirty, with hard beds.

Women needed the vote, Susan now told the crowds who flocked to hear her, to have the power to make laws correcting social evils that afflicted them. They needed to win equal legal standing with their husbands; the right to divorce brutal and drunken husbands; the right to testify in court in their own defense; the right to equal education and jobs, without which many women were forced into prostitution to survive.

Susan was compelled to interrupt her 1876 tour when her brother Daniel was shot and seriously wounded in Kansas. She rushed to be with him, and for nine weeks sat by his bedside nursing him. When he recovered, she went to join her old suffragette friend of thirty years, Lucretia Mott, who was dying. She nursed Lucretia for a month until the end came.

The next year, Susan presented to the Senate petitions for woman's suffrage she had gathered in twenty-six states, signed by over 10,000 people. Sitting in the Senate gallery, she was humiliated by the senators' reactions to her petitions on the floor. Laughing, they dismissed the petitions contemptuously as a preposterous joke. Undeterred, she introduced her constitutional amendment into every session of Congress from that year on.

In 1880, Susan moved into Elizabeth's New Jersey home to write with her a monumental history of the woman suffrage movement. The history took five years to write. Susan declared restlessly, "I love to make history but hate to write it." She escaped as often as she could to continue active crusading.

She went abroad for nine months in 1883 to try to create an international woman suffrage organization. Upon her return, the *Cleveland Leader* noted, "She is sixty-three, but looks just the same as twenty years ago. There is perhaps an extra wrinkle in her face, a little more silver in her hair, but her blue eyes are just as bright, her mouth as serious and her step as active as when she was forty. She would attract attention in any crowd."

When three volumes of *The History of Woman Suffrage* were completed in 1885, Susan and Elizabeth offered a set to the librarians at Vassar College. It was refused. Even at that point, no great importance was attached to the women's crusade for the vote.

One day, Susan and Elizabeth attended a Washington, DC, church to hear the president of Howard University, an all-black college, deliver a sermon. They gasped when he declared, "The recent convention of woman suffragists gave evidence of atheism and immorality." Afterwards, they went up to speak to him.

"Doctor," Susan said, "your mother, if you have one, should lay you across her knee and give you a good spanking for that sermon." But Elizabeth added quickly, "Oh, no, allow me to congratulate you. I have been trying for years to make women understand that the worst enemy they have is in the pulpit, and you have illustrated the truth of it!"

ELEVEN

By January, 1887, woman suffrage organizations had grown so large and influential that the Senate at last felt compelled to vote on the Anthony Amendment. Still, only sixteen senators voted in favor, with thirty-four opposed. An apprehensive twenty-six stayed away from the session, fearing to vote for or against.

That rebuff finally drove the two rival suffrage organizations, the National and the American, to merge into one more powerful force. They united as the National American Woman Suffrage Association (NAWSA). Susan declined the office of president so that Elizabeth could be elected. Susan accepted the vice presidency. Two years later when the aging Elizabeth retired, Susan was unanimously elected in her place.

In 1888, Susan's European trip five years earlier bore fruit. Delegates from seven nations met in Washington to form the International Council of Women, presided over by Susan. President Grover Cleveland held a reception for them at the White House. Susan attended draped in a black dress and the signature red silk shawl that won her instant recognition everywhere she went.

She was eulogized by Frances E. Willard, head of the Women's Christian Temperance Union. "I remember when I was dreadfully afraid of Susan, and Lucy, too," Mrs. Willard confessed. "But now I love and honor them, and I cannot put into words my sense of what it means to me to have the blessing of these women who have made it possible for more timid ones like myself to come forward and take our part in the world's work. If they had not. . . pioneered the way, we should not have dared to come."

Susan and Elizabeth were influential in persuading a number of universities to enroll women for the first time. But despite such successes, Susan felt frustrated by the majority of American women's aloofness to her crusades.

"It is the disheartening part of my life," she wrote, "that so few women will work for the emancipation of their own half of the race. . . . Very few are capable of seeing that the cause of nine-tenths of all the misfortunes which come to women, and to men, also, lies in the subjection of women."

She kept urging the importance of forcing a vote on Congress every year to keep the women's rights issues alive.

In 1890, Amelia Bloomer and her husband celebrated their golden anniversary. Susan cited the occasion as "one of the strongest proofs of the falseness of the charge brought against our movement. . . that the condition of equality of political rights for the wife will cause inharmony and disruption of the marriage bond. To the contrary, such conditions of perfect equality are the best helps to make for peace and harmony. . . ."

At the World's Fair in Chicago in 1893, Susan's International Council developed a World's Congress of Representative Women. Her unmistakable presence on the fairgrounds made her a central attraction. Crowds jammed the hall and corridors to hear her speak, greeting her appearance with enthusiastic applause. She told them why women had still not achieved equality with men:

> It is because women have been taught always to work for something else than their own personal freedom. The hardest thing in the world is to organize women for the one purpose of securing their political liberty and political equality.

At age seventy-four, Susan continued to crusade tirelessly in state after state, and to write endless letters and speeches by hand. In one letter to a friend she wrote, "The other day a millionaire who wrote me 'wondered why I didn't have my letters typewritten.' Why, bless him, I never, in all my fifty years of hard work with the pen, had a writing desk with pigeonholes and drawers until my seventieth birthday brought me the present of one, and never had I even a dream of money for a stenographer and typewriter. How little those who have realize the limitations of those who have not."

In 1894, a Washington paper observed, "Spring is not heralded in Washington by the arrival of the robin, but by the appearance of Miss Anthony's red shawl." She continued to be the dominant figure at suffrage conventions, both in the capital and in the states.

A book by Elizabeth, *The Woman's Bible,* appeared in 1895. It scandalized the NAWSA, which passed a resolution disavowing any connection with Elizabeth for questioning the divine inspiration of certain biblical passages derogatory to women.

Susan immediately rushed to her friend's defense.

"The religious persecution of the ages has been carried on under what was claimed to be the command of God," Susan told the NAWSA convention. "I distrust those people who know so well what God wants them to do, because I notice it always coincides with their own desires. . . . This year it is Mrs. Stanton: next year it may be I or one of yourselves, who will be the victim."

Elizabeth was outraged by the repudiation of the organization she and Susan had birthed. She wanted both of them to resign.

"No, my dear," Susan wrote her. "Instead of resigning and leaving those half-fledged chickens without any mother, I think it my duty and the duty of yourself and all the liberals to be at the next convention and try to reverse this miserable narrow action."

Susan told one reporter, "The Bible was written by men, and therefore its reference to women reflects the light in which they were regarded in those days." She also noted that since almost all historians were men, history books invariably recorded the noble deeds of men, but rarely of women.

Another reporter sought her views on the reappearance of the bloomer costume, which many women cyclists had adopted.

"It would be quite out of good taste as well as good sense," Susan observed, "for a woman to go to her daily work with trailing skirts, flowing sleeves, fringes and laces; and certainly, if women ride the bicycle or climb mountains, they should don a costume which will permit them the use of their legs. It is very

Above, an 1897 cartoon celebrates the twenty-eighth annual convention of the National American Woman Suffrage Association. Elizabeth Cady Stanton is pictured holding the controversial *Women's Bible*. Utah and Wyoming are represented as the two states which had granted women the vote. *Below*, suffragettes march down New York's Fifth Avenue in 1913; their signs give a state-by-state accounting of the extent of woman suffrage.

funny that it is ever and always the men who are troubled about the propriety of the woman's costume."

In an 1896 interview, Susan declared, "I'll tell you what I think of bicycling. I think it has done more to emancipate woman than any one thing in the world. I rejoice every time I see a woman ride by on a wheel. It gives her a feeling of self-reliance and independence the moment she takes her seat; and away she goes, the picture of untrammelled womanhood."

TWELVE

California suffragettes begged for Susan's help in passing a state woman suffrage amendment in 1896. She whipped up support for it by touring the state with a young protégé, Anna Howard Shaw. The campaign proved so strenuous that Susan collapsed upon returning east. Elizabeth wrote her, "I never realized how desolate the world would be to me without you until I heard of your sudden illness."

Although weaker now at seventy-nine, Susan did not hesitate to head the US delegation to the International Council of Women meeting in London. She found that in England, as in the US, the burden of the fight for suffrage had passed from mothers to daughters. Susan was hailed and cheered as a heroine wherever she appeared. "The day will come," she predicted to the world delegates, "when man will recognize woman as his peer, not only at the fireside but in the councils of the nation."

In February, 1900, Susan finally laid down the burden of leading the NAWSA. She told the younger leaders succeeding her, "I want to see you all at work, while I am alive, so I can scold if you do not do it well."

She wrote Elizabeth in 1902, "It is fifty-one years since we first met and we have been busy through every one of them, stirring up the world to recognize the rights of women. . . . These strong, courageous, capable young women will take our place and complete our work. There is an army of them where we were but a handful. . . ."

She planned to visit Elizabeth in November to celebrate her old friend's eighty-seventh birthday. But two weeks before that day a telegram arrived with news of Elizabeth's death. When reporters sought Susan's comment, she could only whisper with tears in her eyes, "I am too crushed to speak."

They had often disagreed, with Elizabeth determined to battle for wide social reform, while Susan believed that this would follow after women were given the vote, so that suffrage should be their single-minded crusade. Yet they had always been the dearest of personal friends as well as comrades-in-arms in the struggle for equality before the law.

Susan testified before a Senate committee on behalf of the Anthony Amendment for the last time in 1904. The eighty-four-year-old Susan reminded the stolid-faced solons wistfully, "I shall not be able to come much longer. . . . We have waited. We stood aside for the Negro, we waited for the millions of immigrants. . . ." Yet educated women were still being denied the vote. "How long," she demanded, "will this injustice, this outrage, continue?"

In May of that year, Susan attended an International Council of Women in Berlin. Her entrance was greeted with a standing ovation. One Berlin paper declared, "The Americans call her 'Aunt Susan.' She is *our* 'Aunt Susan,' too!" The International Council called her "Susan B. Anthony of the World."

Meeting Empress Victoria August of Germany, Susan urged her to speak to Emperor William to raise the status of German women. The Empress smiled, "The gentlemen are very slow to comprehend this great movement."

In 1905, Susan travelled to Portland, Oregon, for a women's rights convention. She was greeted at railroad stations along the way by crowds who cheered her and showered her with flowers.

"This is rather different," Susan told them, smiling, "from the receptions I used to get fifty years ago!"

Susan B. Anthony, *right,* and Elizabeth Cady Stanton—partners in the fight
to win women the vote for fifty years.

She still had her feuds with the White House. When ex-President Cleveland scoffed at woman suffrage in a *Ladies' Home Journal* article, Susan told reporters acidly, "I would think that Grover Cleveland was about the last person to talk about the sanctity of the home and woman's sphere." Cleveland had acknowledged having fathered a child out of wedlock.

She also crossed swords with President Theodore Roosevelt in November, 1905. In a personal meeting, she urged him to recommend her woman suffrage amendment to Congress. He replied evasively that the public knew he had recommended it as governor of New York. But Susan persisted, pointing out that he had never uttered a word of endorsement since becoming president.

"They have no cause to think I have changed my mind," he replied. He refused to use his influence in Congress.

Susan spoke at her final convention in Baltimore in January, 1906. She ended by encouraging the delegates with the firm conviction that had sustained her all her life:

"Failure is impossible!"

At age eighty-six, sensing that the end was coming, Susan sent for her chosen successor, Anna Shaw, who rushed to Rochester. Susan made her promise to keep leading the NAWSA and to carry on the fight for woman suffrage. "Take your stand and hold it," Susan urged, "then let come what will, and receive blows like a good soldier."

On March 13, 1906, as Anna held her hand, Susan died.

Susan Anthony's life's work finally bore fruit fourteen years later with the passage of the Nineteenth Amendment—the Susan Anthony Amendment—giving women the vote.

Anna, who became the first woman ordained as a Methodist minister, wrote, "To me she was an unceasing inspiration—the torch that illuminated my life."

In 1950, Susan B. Anthony was posthumously elected to the Hall of Fame for Great Americans.

Margaret Sanger

1879–1966

"I could not escape from the facts of their misery."

ONE

On a fiercely hot July day in 1912, a pretty, auburn-haired public health nurse hurried through New York's teeming Lower East Side on an emergency call from a doctor. It was not the first time Mrs. Margaret Sanger, thirty-three, had had to attend a desperate woman with too many children who had seriously injured herself by a self-induced abortion.

She found Mrs. Sadie Sachs, a slight twenty-eight-year-old Russian immigrant, hemorrhaging severely. Margaret helped the doctor stop the bleeding, which took several hours. But it took three weeks for the patient to recover, with Margaret's aid. As Margaret prepared to leave, Sadie asked her wanly, "Another thing like this will finish me, I suppose?"

Margaret relayed her fear to the doctor. He told Sadie bluntly that another pregnancy might cost her her life.

"I know, doctor," she nodded, then added hesitantly, "But what can I do to prevent it?"

"You want to have your cake and eat it, too, do you? Well, it can't be done." Picking up his bag to leave, he grinned wryly. "Tell Jake to sleep on the roof!"

Margaret felt herself grow tense with rage at the doctor's insensitivity, treating the poor woman's plight as a joke. After he had left, Sadie broke down and wept on Margaret's shoulder. She sobbed, "Please tell me the secret and I'll never breathe it to a soul. Please!"

But Margaret felt helpless to give Sadie the information she needed. Condoms were one way to prevent pregnancy, but they were expensive for poor people, not always reliable, and most husbands refused to be bothered with them. Douching after intercourse by the woman was a questionable preventive. And in cold water tenements, even women who knew about it were too embarrassed to sneak down a hall, douche bag in hand, to the only toilet.

A few months later, Jake frantically summoned Margaret again. Sadie, pregnant once more, had desperately tried to abort herself a second time. This time she was bleeding so badly that she died. Agonized, Jake tore his hair as he paced the room sobbing, "My God! My God! My God!"

Over twenty years later, Margaret wrote about that night, a turning point in her life: "I knew I could not go on merely nursing, allowing mothers to suffer and die. . . . I went to bed knowing that no matter what it might cost . . . I was resolved to do something to change the destiny of mothers whose miseries were vast as the sky."

That change would require breaking society's taboo against investigating and distributing effective birth control information to women who needed practical knowledge to prevent unwanted pregnancies. Margaret never dreamed that her pursuit of that goal would result in the sacrifice of her marriage, and guilt over the loss of one of her children.

Her determination was spurred by the memory of her own mother, worn out after bearing eleven children and dying at forty-eight of tuberculosis. Margaret was also driven by her knowledge that in New York City alone over 100,000 women a year were estimated to seek illegal abortions. No one knew how many women died or were crippled as a result.

Two years after Sadie Sachs's death, and still haunted by her memory, Margaret began her crusade. She had to defy federal, state, and local laws, for which she was thrown in jail eight times. She also had to face the condemnation of the medical profession, churches, the press, and even liberal reformers. Against such odds, the red-haired, fiery little Irishwoman fought a lifelong battle on behalf of women around the world.

TWO

She was born Margaret Higgins in Corning, New York, on September 14, 1883, of Irish parents. Her nonconformist father, Michael, was a Catholic-born Socialist and atheist who eked out a bare living by carving angels and saints on tombstones.

His stubborn sponsorship of notorious atheist and Socialist speakers in Corning cost him so many commissions that his children grew up impoverished. "Our existence was like that of any artist's family," Margaret recalled. "Chickens today and feathers tomorrow."

As for her mother, Margaret wrote, "Though never strong, Mother was always busy sewing, cleaning, doing this and that for the ever-increasing family. I wondered at her patience and her love for him."

Once her father arranged for the atheist Robert G. Ingersoll to speak at the Corning Town Hall. Margaret and the older children were taken to hear him. But the mayor padlocked the door. The meeting was broken up by hurled fruit and vegetables.

That, Margaret recalled, was "my first experience of rage directed against those holding views which were contrary to accepted ones." The Higgins youngsters became known as "children of the Devil,"and were forced to endure the jeers and ostracism of classmates. These experiences strengthened Margaret's ability to withstand later torments as an adult.

One childhood adventure foreshadowed the reckless daring and courage that was to characterize Margaret as a woman rebel. The Higgins children were forbidden to cross alone a high railroad bridge which had widely spaced ties a child could fall through. Margaret felt dizzy and frightened whenever her father took her across. One day, challenging herself to conquer that fear, she tried to cross the bridge by herself.

Halfway over, she heard a train coming. Panicked, she stumbled and fell, dropping between two ties. But her arms flashed out around the ties, leaving her dangling in space. The bridge shook as the train roared over her. She prayed that the engineer would not release hot steam from the locomotive as it passed. In shock from the ordeal, Margaret hung there numbly until a family friend fishing in the river observed her predicament and rescued her.

It did not escape Margaret's notice that most wealthy families in Corning had fewer children and enjoyed more pleasure-filled lives than her own family. In contrast, most families that lived at a poverty level had lots of children. Was the key to a better family life the ability to limit a woman's babies to just those she really wanted and the family could afford?

Margaret's father encouraged his children to be independent, socially aware thinkers. "You have no right to material comforts," he taught them, "without giving back to society the benefit of your honest experience." When they left home, he advised each one, "Leave the world better because you, my child, have dwelt in it."

One day, encouraged by her mother to recite the Lord's Prayer, Margaret reached the line, "Give us this day our daily bread." Her father interrupted, "Why are you asking God for bread? Is he a baker?" He told her to reason things out for herself. "Thereafter," Margaret wrote, "I began to question what I had previously taken for granted."

Despite her admiration for her father, Margaret's childhood, reared as she was in poverty and community hostility, was unhappy. Later, as an adult, she wrote, "When I'm passing through Corning at night by train, my body knows I'm there without seeing it. I actually become sick to my stomach."

She managed to get to Claverack College, a private boarding school, by waiting on tables and washing dishes. After three years, she was forced to return home because her mother was dying of TB. Margaret took over running the household and looking after her younger siblings. Watching her mother die filled Margaret with bitter thoughts about marriage, particularly a wife's submission to exhausting pregnancy after pregnancy.

To nurse her mother more effectively, she borrowed medical books from the local doctor. Studying about tuberculosis made her interested in medicine. She began to dream about becoming a physician, an unlikely aspiration for a poor girl in an era when most women's goals were limited to becoming teachers, typists, or nurses.

After her mother died, her father seemed to go to pieces, becoming irrational. Margaret fought with him constantly, blaming him for her mother's early death because he'd made her mother pregnant eighteen times. Her enraged father once locked her out of the house, fueling her determination to leave.

In 1900, she won acceptance as a probationer nurse at White Plains Hospital for room, board, and a token salary. Night duty brought some harrowing experiences with psychotic patients. One patient lunged at her with a knife. Gripping his wrist, she escaped death only because illness had left him weak. Margaret learned subsequently that he was a gangster who had been implicated in five murders.

Another deranged patient asked her for a drink, then knocked her ten feet against a wall. He choked her until an orderly dashed to her rescue.

At a dance for the hospital staff, Margaret met Socialist William Sanger, twenty-nine, a doctor's guest. Immediately smitten by her flashing blue eyes, mass of reddish hair, vivacity, and soft voice, he began to pursue her ardently. When he urged her to marry him, Margaret put him off, determined to complete her nursing apprenticeship first.

Often called out in the middle of the night on maternity cases, she frequently had to deliver the baby herself when the doctor was late. Many poor mothers begged her for advice about avoiding subsequent pregnancies. She would refer them to the doctor, who would only shrug. Margaret grew more certain than ever that there was something seriously wrong with compelling women to be mothers against their will, especially those with more babies than they could feed and clothe properly or those too ill to look after the families they already had.

And was it fair to the babies themselves, she mused, to let them come into the world unwanted, with less chance of the loving care and opportunities all children deserved?

But knowledge of birth control techniques was limited to a specialized few. The very mention of the subject was almost universally taboo. When Margaret ventured to discuss it with her father, that unconventional freethinker sighed, "Margaret, can't you find some other subject in the world to talk about besides the bedroom?" Contraception was unmentionable, immoral, illegal. It was a federal crime merely to send information about it through the mails.

THREE

On August 18, 1902, Margaret finally let Bill Sanger sweep her off her feet into marriage. "That beast of a man William," she wrote to her sister Mary, "took me out for a drive last Monday and drove me to a minister's residence and married me. I wept with anger and would not look at him, for it was so unexpected. I had an old blue dress on, and I looked horrid. Now the only thing is to make the best of it. . . . He is the loveliest of men but I am mad at him. . . . I am very sorry to have had this thing occur, but yet I am very, very happy."

They had three children, who were often looked after by her mother-in-law as Margaret pursued her nursing career. She often joined Bill in attending Socialist meetings. Through him she met and entertained leading radical labor leaders like Eugene Debs and Big Bill Haywood, anarchists like Emma Goldman, famous liberals like journalists Lincoln Steffens and John Reed, and famous lawyers like Clarence Darrow.

Stirred by the ferment of such powerful left-wing company, Margaret joined the Socialist Party. "Almost without realizing it," she wrote later, "you become a 'comrade' or 'fellow worker,' like the primitive Christian, a member of a secret order. . . . One had hardly any social standing at all in radical circles unless one had . . . brushed up against the police or had served at least a few days in jail."

One day, a Socialist speaker scheduled to talk to a group of working women on labor problems had to cancel, and Margaret was asked to substitute. "I was frightened—thoroughly so," she recalled later. "I could not eat my supper." She finally decided to talk about a subject she knew more about—sex and reproduction. Her talk was enthusiastically received.

She was then persuaded to give a series of similar lectures, followed by a question period. The *Socialist Call* asked her to compile the questions and answers into a column under the title, *What Every Mother Should Know.* Appearing first in November, 1912, the column proved so popular that the *Call* announced a second series by Margaret to be called *What Every Girl Should Know.*

The first column, readers were told, would deal with sexual disease. But when the next issue appeared, the *Call* left its women's page blank except for these words in large type:

WHAT EVERY GIRL SHOULD KNOW

NOTHING!

BY ORDER OF THE POST-OFFICE DEPARTMENT

That was Margaret's first run-in with censorship. The "anti-vice" Comstock Law of 1873 had been signed by President Grant. It had included an amendment appointing whiskered little Anthony Comstock, self-righteous head of the New York Society for the Suppression of Vice, as special anti-obscenity agent of the Post Office. He was given authority to open any mail and censor "every obscene, lewd, lascivious or filthy book, pamphlet, picture, paper, letter, writing, print or other publication of an indecent character."

Comstock considered any attempt to warn teenage girls about the need to prevent syphilis obscene. The *Call* was forbidden to run any more sex-related articles by Margaret.

In 1912, poorly paid Italian textile workers in Lawrence, Massachusetts, went out on strike. The Socialists in New York asked Margaret, as a nurse, to head a committee to go to Lawrence and give physical exams to the strikers' children. She was then to bring them back to New York to stay and be cared for by Italian Socialist families for as long as the strike lasted.

But Lawrence police, acting for the mill owners, used violence to try to prevent the departure of the children. A congressional committee investigated. Margaret was called to testify on how undernourished, raggedly clad, and unhealthy most of the children were. Her testimony, reported in the press, helped create public sympathy for the strikers. The mill owners finally felt compelled to meet the strikers' demands.

Margaret went back to work for the Visiting Nurses Association of the Lower East Side. This association, run by the Henry Street Settlement House, sent nurses out to take care of poor patients. Margaret also took private jobs that brought her into wealthy homes as a midwife and baby nurse for women who preferred to deliver babies at home.

Unlike the mothers she attended in the slum tenements, the well-to-do mothers were often having only a first or second baby. Both mothers and babies received a great amount of celebration, gifts, and care.

Margaret could not help contrasting the dramatic difference between wanted and unwanted babies. The former began life with a distinct advantage, the latter with a handicap. Margaret grew more and more convinced that babies deserved to be planned for by loving parents, not regarded as tragic misfortunes by parents with too many children and too few resources.

Most poor women she helped, often worn out by the age of thirty, continually begged Margaret for the "secret" of preventing unwanted pregnancies. In every slum tenement she visited, neighbors would bring her gifts, hoping to bribe her into revealing some hushed-up method to prevent continuous childbearing.

But she could only tell them about the condom and incomplete intercourse. This knowledge was of little use to the wives because, Margaret wrote later, "it placed the burden of responsibility upon the husband, a burden which he seldom assumed."

What was needed, she knew, was a contraceptive method that women could control themselves. Yet even in telling women what she did know, Margaret was aware that she was breaking the Comstock law. She brooded over "men's law" that forbade teaching the means of fertility control to women. Doctors called excessive fertility a social problem. Social workers called it a medical problem. Meanwhile, thousands of wretched women followed old wives' remedies in seeking to end unwanted pregnancies, employing dangerous or useless techniques which left many dead or permanently crippled.

"They claimed my thoughts night and day," Margaret wrote sadly. "One by one these women, with their worried, sad, pensive and aging faces would marshal themselves before me in my dreams, sometimes appealingly, sometimes accusingly. I could not escape from the facts of their misery."

FOUR

Margaret tried to obtain effective female contraceptive information from several friendly doctors. They told her that such knowledge might exist somewhere, but even if they knew or if she discovered it, the law would still ban any transmission of it.

Many druggists were even serving prison terms for having sold condoms or just rubber syringes used in douching.

Undeterred, Margaret haunted medical and public libraries searching for the information. But all the books had been effectively sanitized. She was only able to find and read *The Psychology of Sex* by British sexologist Havelock Ellis. To her disappointment, however, it dealt only with sexual abnormalities. She agreed with Ellis's view that sex was a spiritual, divine urge, thus sacred. But how could a sacred urge so often produce misery for a married couple?

When Margaret's daughter Peggy developed polio, her husband Bill implied that it was the result of Margaret's neglect because of her obsession with the contraception problem. Their marriage became strained.

Big Bill Haywood suggested to Margaret that she take her quest to France. There, he told her, some kind of limitation of family size had been going on for generations. She decided to go. Maybe the secret she yearned to discover could be found in Europe. Bill agreed to the trip, feeling that a holiday in France might save their troubled marriage. He also hoped to pursue an earlier ambition to be an artist by studying in Paris.

They left for the Continent with the children in October, 1913. In Paris, Margaret found no laws against birth control, and abortions were carried out legally by doctors. Most poor families consequently were small, with children invariably cherished. French wives used such female contraceptive methods as suppositories and douches. When these methods failed, abortion was common.

The more Margaret pursued her quest, and the more Bill involved himself in art, the further apart they grew. She asked for a divorce. Bill stayed behind in Paris to paint while Margaret and the children sailed for home.

Thinking about what she had learned in France, Margaret wrote later, "I knew something must be done to rescue those women who were voiceless. Someone had to express with white hot intensity the conviction that they must be empowered to decide for themselves when they should fulfill the supreme function of motherhood. They had to be made aware of how they were being shackled, and aroused to mutiny."

Calling a conference of young feminists, she founded an organization to promote the cause of contraception. One supporter suggested they name their crusade "birth control." Margaret liked the term, and the National Birth Control League was born. One of its objectives was to educate a hostile medical profession, winning over doctors to the cause despite the law.

To advance the movement, Margaret published a feminist magazine called *The Woman Rebel,* with the motto, "No Gods, No Masters." Her first issue in March, 1914, featured denunciations of marriage, property laws favoring men, established religion, capitalism, and laws against contraceptive information.

A woman's duty, Margaret wrote, was "to look the world in the face with a go-to-hell look in the eyes . . . to speak and act in defiance of convention." She promised that an early feature would offer specific information on birth control for girls fourteen to eighteen. "In this present chaos of sex atmosphere," she declared, "it is difficult for the girl of this uncertain age to know just what to do, or really what constitutes clean living without prudishness."

That was enough for Comstock. The Post Office informed Margaret that her March issue was banned from the mails.

"To me it was outrageous," she declared indignantly, "that information regarding motherhood, which was so generally called sacred, should be classed with pornography!"

She and some assistants managed to post copies, a few at a time in different mail drops, escaping the censor's vigilance. Thousands of enthusiastic letters from readers poured in, some from leading European feminists, urging Margaret on.

In the April issue she wrote defiantly, " *The Woman Rebel* feels proud that the Post Office authorities did not approve of her.

She shall blush with shame if ever she be approved of by official-ism or 'Comstockism.'"

When this issue, too, was banned, Margaret flouted Comstock in the May issue with an article warning of the dangers of abortion brought about by the failure to use birth control. Now the postmaster general, prodded by Comstock, denounced her paper as "indecent, lewd, lascivious and obscene." Postal authorities seized all copies of *The Woman Rebel.*

On August 25, 1914, Margaret was indicted on nine counts of sending birth control information through the mails. If found guilty, she faced up to forty-five years in prison. Most of the press approved of her indictment.

The *Pittsburgh Sun* called *The Woman Rebel* "a mass of dirty slush. . . . The whole thing is nauseating!"

FIVE

Despite her indictment, Margaret stubbornly continued to publish *The Woman Rebel.* In the September-October issue she wrote, "While practically every thinker of the civilized world is now accepting birth control, the arch-hypocritical government of the United States is not."

To defy the law further, she wrote a pamphlet giving specific birth control advice she had learned in France, with formulas and drawings. She called it *Family Limitation.* But twenty print-ers refused to risk printing it. Margaret finally found one who agreed to do it after hours behind locked doors.

She managed to get bundles of the pamphlet delivered to radical and Socialist locals around the country. They were to offer the pamphlets for sale as her defiance to Comstock if she were imprisoned.

Margaret's father Michael was at first shocked at his daughter's growing emergence as the leading American champion of sexual information. He blamed this on her training as a nurse.

Her brash behavior, he thought, was a form of hysteria, the sign of a nervous breakdown. But after reading a few issues of *The Woman Rebel,* he changed his mind.

"Your mother would be alive today," he admitted to her somberly, "if we had just known all this then!"

Margaret's lawyer urged her to plead guilty, assuring her he could probably get her off with only a fine. She refused, declaring that she had deliberately violated the law in order to challenge it in court. "I was trying to prove," she wrote later, "the law was wrong, not I."

But she worried about what might happen to her children if she went to prison. Friends then offered to look after them for her until Bill could return from France.

"I was not afraid of the penitentiary," she recalled. "I was not afraid of anything except being misunderstood."

She asked for a postponement of her trial to give her time to prepare an adequate defense. The judge denied her request. Indignant, Margaret "postponed" the trial herself by leaving on a midnight train for Montreal in October, 1914. Writing to tell the judge that she would notify him when she returned, she defiantly enclosed a copy of *Family Limitation.*

Anarchist friends in Canada forged a passport for her. Under the name of "Bertha Watson" she took off for England. Sending coded cables to the groups holding bundles of her pamphlet, Margaret asked that they be sold for a quarter each, the money to be sent to her in London care of American Express.

Her flight accomplished what the Post Office and Comstock dreaded most—widespread publicity about the censorship of birth control. Meanwhile, Margaret set out in London to find out everything she could about birth control there that might help her defend herself, as well as add to her knowledge.

She was invited to tea by Dr. C. V. Drysdale and his wife, leaders of the British movement for population control. Their secretary wrote later, "We awaited with curiosity, and also a little apprehension, the visit of *The Woman Rebel*, but we were hardly prepared for the surprise given us by the soft-voiced, gentle-mannered, altogether charming 'rebel' who tapped at the door."

The Drysdales directed Margaret to the British Museum for studies of the British population control movement, which had long since defeated British obscenity laws.

She was fascinated to discover that as early as 1841 Queen Victoria herself had indicated her approval of birth control. Shortly after her marriage, the Queen had written to her uncle, King Leopold of Belgium, "I think you will see the great inconvenience a *large* family would be to us all, and particularly to the country, independent of the hardship and inconvenience to myself. Men never think, at least seldom think, what a hard task it is for us women to go through this very often."

Margaret also came across a book by an early American reformer, Robert Dale, the first to explain why contraception was necessary in his *Moral Philosophy*. It also described the known methods of that day. Dr. Charles Knowlton of Massachusetts had read it, experimented with methods of his own, and written a second book on the subject. Although he had published it anonymously in 1832, Massachusetts authorities had traced the book to him.

Arrested, he had been tried and sentenced to three months at hard labor. After that, American doctors had been unwilling to risk their careers or jail by giving contraceptive advice.

The Drysdales introduced Margaret to Havelock Ellis, whose controversial works on sex she had read earlier. They became intimate friends. Ellis and the Drysdales persuaded Margaret to forget about Socialism, and concentrate on making birth control a "respectable" subject in order to educate Americans and change the restrictive Comstock laws.

Ellis convinced Margaret to broaden her mission, from working solely for the good of mothers to working for the good of the world by helping limit world population to available resources. Margaret fell in love with him, even though she was still officially married. She wrote Bill that she considered their marriage at an end.

Through Ellis and the Drysdales she met famous British writers like George Bernard Shaw, H. G. Wells, and Arnold Bennett, as well as leading English physicians. Charmed by the enthusiastic American, they were impressed with her dedication to maternal welfare despite the opposition of the American government.

Margaret was stunned by news that her husband, returning to New York from Paris, had been arrested for giving a secret police agent who had requested it a copy of her pamphlet. Comstock himself had offered to free Bill if he would reveal the whereabouts of his wife. Spurning the offer, Bill had been thrown in jail. At his trial, the judge fumed at him, "Your crime violates not only the laws of the State but the laws of God."

"I would rather be in jail with my convictions," Bill replied defiantly, "than be free at a loss of my manhood and self-respect. This court can't intimidate me!" He was marched off to jail amid enthusiastic courtroom cheers and applause.

From jail he wrote Margaret urging her to stay in England because if she returned home to face trial, she was likely to get a far stiffer sentence than his.

SIX

To increase her knowledge of birth control, Margaret went to Holland. Here birth control clinics had been operating successfully for thirty-eight years. In 1910, Queen Wilhelmina had awarded Holland's birth control league a medal of honor and a royal charter. Here at last Margaret learned some useful specific techniques of female contraception. She also found evidence that they had sharply reduced Holland's rate of both maternal and infant deaths to the lowest in the world. The US at the time had one of the highest maternity death rates.

Holland gave Margaret the idea for developing a chain of birth control clinics throughout the United States, each staffed with doctors. Their purpose would not be the elimination of pregnancies, but the proper spacing of children as married couples wished to add to their families.

Some American friends wrote Margaret urging her to return home now because public opinion seemed to be more receptive to birth control. Other friends warned, however, that if she came back she would be tried promptly and jailed. But Margaret, realizing that with Bill in jail, their children would need her, sailed for home in September, 1915. Even as she did, she read press statements by Comstock that for writing *Family Limitation* Margaret deserved a lifetime in prison at hard labor.

A surprise awaited her arrival in New York. Her chief tormentor and enemy, Anthony Comstock, had just died. But that did not stop her trial from going forward. Margaret also learned that during her absence her National Birth Control League had been reorganized. Its new leader, Mary Ware Dennett, disapproved of Margaret's defiance of the law to force a test, and refused to allow the League to support her.

Once more, Margaret's lawyer urged her to plead guilty and promise to respect the law in the future, so that he could keep her from going to jail. "I couldn't promise that," she replied firmly. "The law is there. Something must happen to it. Imparting birth control information is not obscene. If I have done nothing obscene, I cannot plead guilty."

Not wanting a lawyer to evade the issue in order to win an acquittal, Margaret decided to defend herself. She wrote afterward, "I determined to remain and fight the case out in the courts, depending upon the common sense, the intelligence and understanding of public opinion for the support I needed."

Her supporters, now a steadily growing number, published an open letter to President Woodrow Wilson. Signed by celebrities like Arnold Bennett and H. G. Wells, it protested the persecution of Margaret for circulating information on birth control, "allowed in every civilized country except the United States."

A new crisis arose for Margaret in November when her five-year-old daughter Peggy, who had been stricken with polio, died of pneumonia. Margaret was filled with remorse and guilt for having been absent from her children, blaming herself for Peggy's death. Thousands of her supporters sent their sympathy.

As the day of her trial approached, her journalist friend John Reed suggested that Margaret ought to try to dispel the impression that she was a tough woman crusader. He persuaded her to be photographed in a plain dress, looking feminine and beautiful, with her two sons. This photo, appearing in hundreds of papers, won her the support of many important people who had been wary of her revolutionary image. The judge sitting in her case was showered with telegrams and letters demanding her acquittal.

The night before the trial, a dinner in her honor was held at the Brevoort Hotel, attended by famous political pundit Walter Lippmann; Senator Bob La Follette's daughter, Katharine Houghton, who was the mother of Katharine Hepburn; society leader Mrs. Ogden Reid; and two New York City health commissioners.

In her speech to the distinguished guests, Margaret said, "Women from time immemorial have tried to avoid unwanted motherhood. *We all know* the tribe of professional abortionists which has sprung up and profited by this terrible misfortune. . . . I found wise men, sages and scientists discussing birth control among themselves. But . . . they did not influence or affect . . . the working classes and the disinherited. . . . How could I awaken public opinion to this tremendous problem? I might have taken up a policy of . . . conservatism, but would I

Margaret Sanger, *left*, appears with supporters from both sides of the Atlantic: British author H. G. Wells and Katharine Houghton Hepburn, one of the founders of Connecticut's Planned Parenthood.

have got a hearing? . . . I felt myself in the position of one who has discovered that a house is on fire, and I found that it was up to me to shout out the warning!"

The guests applauded enthusiastically, and many rose to pledge Margaret their financial support in her crusade, The affair made impressive newspaper headlines. Mary Ware Dennett, surprised by Margaret's support from such prominent citizens, announced that the National Birth Control League had decided after all to stand behind its founder.

The courtroom was jammed the next day with both wealthy and poor supporters. The district attorney, realizing he had a tiger by the tail, asked for a postponement of the trial. When the *Pictorial Review* took a poll of its readers, it reported that 97 percent favored birth control. The government then suddenly and discreetly dismissed its charges against Margaret.

"We are determined not to let Mrs. Sanger become a martyr if we can help it," the DA declared. "We are also not the least bit interested in having a public debate on sex theories at this time."

The torrent of publicity made Margaret an important national figure. The issue of birth control had finally been brought out of the closet. "Margaret Sanger," Walter Lippmann wrote, "has kicked the subject clear across to the Pacific."

But she still had not achieved her objective—overturning the laws still in effect against providing birth control information and contraceptives. In the spring of 1916, she set about confronting the government with a new challenge. She began to initiate the plan she had conceived in Holland to create a chain of birth control clinics all over the country. They were to be staffed by doctors and nurses "who will instruct women in the things they need to know."

She organized support for the clinics by travelling and lecturing in state after state for three months. In St. Louis, a crowd of 2,000 gathered to hear her, but at the instigation of local priests they were locked out of the lecture hall she had booked.

Undeterred, Margaret climbed on the seat of her car and began speaking to the crowd in the street. A policeman grabbed her arm and forced her to stop.

"We're not in St. Louis," she cried. "We're in Russia!"

In Portland, Oregon, she was arrested along with supporters who assisted her in distributing copies of *Family Limitation* at a public meeting. Hundreds of women marched to jail behind them, demanding that they be arrested, too. The embarrassed sheriff had to lock the jail entrance against them. When Margaret and the others refused offers of bail from supporters, they were jailed overnight. She and a woman doctor, Marie Equi, were given suspended sentences, while the others received ten-dollar fines.

SEVEN

Margaret returned home exhausted from her tour. She also felt frustrated because, despite her crusade, almost all doctors were still afraid to endorse birth control. To open the first American birth control clinic in New York, she knew she would need a doctor on staff. An idea occurred to her that might protect a doctor from prosecution for providing contraceptives or birth control information.

Section 1145 of the New York Penal Code allowed doctors to prescribe contraceptives "for the cure or prevention of disease," an exception made to protect *men* from venereal disease.

"I wanted the interpretation broadened," Margaret wrote, "with the intent to protect women from ill health as the result of excessive child-bearing, and, equally important, to give them the right to control their own destinies. . . . I believed that if a woman must break the law to establish a right to voluntary motherhood, the law must be broken."

When no woman doctor would risk helping her open a birth control clinic, Margaret enlisted the aid of her younger sister Ethel

Byrne, who was now a registered nurse. They tramped the streets of New York's boroughs seeking inexpensive clinic space. Doors were slammed in their faces when their purpose was known.

Finally, in the Brownsville slum area of Brooklyn they found a sympathetic landlord named Rabinowitz. He rented them two first-floor rooms for fifty dolars a month, and even painted the rooms white for them to make the clinic more "hospital-looking."

Margaret had 5,000 handbills printed in English, Yiddish, and Italian reading:

> MOTHERS—Can you afford to have a large family? Do you want any more children? If not, why do you have them? DO NOT KILL, DO NOT TAKE LIFE, BUT PREVENT. Safe, harmless information can be obtained of trained Nurses, 37 Amboy Street. . . . Tell your friends and neighbors. All mothers welcome. A registration fee of 10 cents entitles any mother to this information.

When the clinic opened its doors, shawled, hatless, careworn mothers clutching handbills formed a line halfway to the corner. They continued to come all day long and into the evening, Protestants, Catholics, and Jews. Every day, the little waiting room was crowded. As the word spread, more and more women came from neighboring states as well.

"If you don't help me," one sweatshop worker with eight children vowed to Margaret, "I'll chop up a glass and swallow it tonight!"

The sisters lectured the women on the basic techniques of contraception, and provided some female contraceptive devices. One grateful mother prophesied that one day there would be a monument raised to Margaret Sanger on the site of the clinic. Complete case histories were kept on the patients, to enable Margaret to write a scientific report on the clinic's work.

Ten days after the clinic had opened, a stony-faced woman pushed her way through the crowded waiting room.

"I'm a police officer," she told Margaret. "You are under arrest."

Outraged, Margaret stormed, "You're no woman! You're a traitress to your sex!"

Three vice squad policemen confiscated the case histories in the clinic files, Margaret's pamphlets, and contraceptive supplies. They also lined up the patients, demanding their names and addresses. Some screamed and others wept until an indignant Margaret shamed the police into letting them leave.

When the police ordered Margaret to enter a patrol wagon, she refused. Eyes flashing, she declared she would rather walk the mile to the station house than sit with the police. In the end they permitted her and Ethel to do so, followed by several policemen, a large crowd of women, reporters, and photographers.

"I stayed overnight at the Raymond Street Jail, and I shall never forget it," Margaret wrote later. "The mattresses were spotted and smelly, the blankets stiff with dirt and grime. The stench nauseated me. I wrapped my coat around me. . . . For endless hours I struggled with roaches and horrible-looking bugs. . . . When a rat jumped up on the bed I cried out involuntarily and sent it scuttling out."

The next afternoon, bail arranged, Margaret returned to the clinic and reopened it. When women reappeared for help, she gave it to them. Police swooped down and arrested her once again. Not only that, they made the landlord sign eviction papers charging Margaret with "maintaining a public nuisance."

She wrote a furious letter to the judge before whom she was to be tried, and released it to the press. "In those birth control cases at which you have presided," she wrote, "you have shown to all thinking men and women an unfailing prejudice, and exposed a mind steeped in the bigotry and intolerance of the Inquisition. To come before you implies conviction."

Margaret won more headlines when the embarrassed judge postponed the case, then passed the "hot potato" to another

In October 1916, Margaret Sanger is arrested for violation of the Comstock Law.

magistrate to try. She used the extended time to round up more important supporters. When she appealed to the New York County Medical Society, they refused to support her right to dispense female birth control information and help. That, Margaret charged wryly, was because male doctors wanted to keep contraception a male prerogative and choice, with women powerless to prevent pregnancy.

In January, 1917, her sister Ethel was tried first, found guilty, and sentenced to thirty days in the workhouse. Ethel promptly went on a hunger strike and made out her will, declaring, "I made up my mind last night to die for the cause. I shall die, if need be, for my sex!"

After Ethel had gone over a hundred hours without food or water, the anxious New York commissioner of correction, Burdette Lewis, ordered her rolled in a blanket while a mixture of milk, eggs, and brandy was poured down her throat forcibly. Ethel became the first woman in American history to be force-fed while in jail. Enraged, Margaret aroused a storm of protest.

She led a delegation to Governor Charles Whitman urging him to pardon Ethel until her case was appealed. He agreed, provided Margaret would assure him that Ethel would stop all birth control work until then. Deeply worried about her sister's health, Margaret gave him that assurance.

EIGHT

On January 29, 1917, as an anxious nation waited to see whether President Wilson would declare war on Germany, Margaret's trial opened. About fifty immigrant women clutched fruit, bread, and babies as they eagerly awaited a chance to help their angel of mercy. One by one they testified how the defendant helped the sick, the desperately poor, the mother who had ten live and three dead children. In their simplicity, they thought they were helping Margaret. Instead, they were proving the district attorney's case against her.

"Margaret Sanger, stand up!"

She faced the bench, pale but calm. Would she, the Court demanded, solemnly promise not to violate the law again?

No, she replied defiantly, she would not. "I can't respect the law as it stands today."

The Brownsville mothers shouted approval. Elite members of the Committee of One Hundred, society women who supported Margaret in her crusade, applauded vigorously.

The judge pounded his gavel angrily. "The judgment of the Court is that you be confined to the workhouse for the period of thirty days!"

"Shame!" cried a spectator. Margaret was led away for the first of eight prison terms she was to serve.

Taken to be fingerprinted, she indignantly refused to cooperate. "I'm a political prisoner," she cried, "not a criminal!" She also prevented a physical examination for the same reason.

"You're one of the fighting kind, are you?" a woman attendant sneered. "Well, we'll soon fix you, young lady!"

She vanished for instructions. When she reappeared, she said with new respect, "Oh, you're Mrs. Sanger. It's all right. Come this way, please." Prison officials obviously had no stomach for any more unfavorable publicity by using force against Margaret.

For one month, she lived in the Queens County penitentiary in Long Island City with female pickpockets, embezzlers, thieves, prostitutes, and drug addicts. Discovering that many were illiterate, she helped them read and write their letters. Some who had heard about her asked her to explain about "sex hygiene."

When Margaret asked permission to do this, the prison matron laughed, "Ah, gwan wid ye. They know bad enough already!" But Margaret persisted and finally won permission.

She also made plans to carry her crusade forward, including an appeal of her case to the highest court possible.

Before she was released on March 6, the warden ordered another effort made to fingerprint her. Margaret fought so vigorously for two hours that police headquarters finally ordered the attempt stopped. As she left the prison, she was cheered by women prisoners waving from the upper windows.

A crowd of supporters, including the Brownsville mothers, greeted Margaret with the revolutionary strains of the "Marseillaise." Then she was whisked off to a luncheon in her honor.

A new publication she had planned before her arrest, *Birth Control Review*, had appeared while she was in prison. With the press increasingly friendly now to her cause, Margaret plunged eagerly back to her crusading work. At the same time, she couldn't shake off feelings of guilt for "robbing my children of time to which they were entitled." But she could not forget the agony of women looking to her for liberation from unwanted pregnancies.

"I can still see them," she sighed, "those poor, weak, wasted, frail women, pregnant year after year like so many automatic breeding machines."

She revised her *Family Limitation* pamphlet, for which she now received two to three hundred requests daily. The requests all contained self-addressed envelopes which Margaret and her helpers would fill and post in a number of different mailboxes. Since all the return envelopes were in different handwriting, post office censors failed to spot the illegal mailing. Margaret and Ethel concealed bundles of the pamphlets under the beds in their apartments.

Margaret's persistent writing, lecturing, and crusading gradually made birth control a popular and respectable topic for public discussion. Her *Birth Control Review* became the official voice of the movement, often featuring articles by such distinguished people as Dr. Karl Menninger of the famous Menninger Clinic, and authors Pearl Buck and Julian Huxley.

To help raise funds for the *Review* and her work, Margaret founded the Birth Control League of New York.

When President Wilson took America into World War I, Margaret denounced his decision in the *Review*. She charged that women were being denied birth control to force them to breed more "cannon fodder," so that old men could wage their wars with youths. A woman, Margaret declared wryly, was used as "a brood animal for the masculine civilizations of the world."

When her case finally reached the New York Court of Appeals in January, 1918, the court decided on a new liberal interpretation of the Comstock Law. Doctors were now authorized to give contraceptive information to a married man *or woman* for "health reasons." This ruling finally opened clinics staffed by doctors, and doctors' offices, to women for birth control help.

Since Margaret and Ethel were nurses, not doctors, however, their conviction by the lower court was upheld.

So now when Margaret answered the thousands of letters that begged her for practical contraceptive advice, she referred them to the nearest physicians who were entitled to provide it.

Ironically, an early article Margaret had written for the *Socialist Call* on venereal disease, which had been censored by the Post Office, was now revived by none other than the government itself. The US Army published it as a precautionary pamphlet for distribution to the soldiers of World War I.

In 1919, Mary Ware Dennett, who had also now taken up the fight for disseminating birth control information nationally, organized the national Voluntary Parenthood League in Washington, DC. Dennett's position was that it should be possible for anyone to dispense this information. Disagreeing, Margaret insisted that only doctors and clinics should offer it. She refused Dennett the cooperation of the New York Birth Control League.

When the war was over, Margaret returned to England almost every year for a lecture tour. She also attended American parties thrown by society supporters, charming wealthy partygoers into offering substantial contributions for her crusade.

At one of these parties, she met J. Noah H. Slee, a South African millionaire, who pursued her doggedly. Divorcing Bill legally in 1920, Margaret agreed to marry Noah, provided he promised her total freedom to continue her campaigns.

She wrote a book called *Woman and the New Race,* published in 1920. In it, she urged labor unions to strike against all laws banning birth control information and help. Such a strike, she pointed out, would win them better lives than they'd get by striking against employers, because wages would go much further in supporting a small family than a large one.

"We must not permit an increase in population we are not prepared for," Margaret wrote, adding, "We must set motherhood free." Her fame by this time brought sales of her book to over 200,000 copies, making it a bestseller.

NINE

In 1921, she founded a rival national organization to Dennett's, the American Birth Control League. To launch it, she organized the first National Birth Control Conference with the theme, "Birth Control! Is It Moral?" An enormous crowd gathered to hear her at the New York Town Hall.

But although the hall was jammed, Margaret herself was blocked from entering by a policeman who told her the meeting was being cancelled, on orders from Archbishop Patrick Hayes.

She managed to slip inside, but was stopped again in front of the stage by another policeman. A huge man suddenly lifted Margaret up bodily, passing her over the officer's head onto the platform. Jumping up beside her, he handed her a bouquet of roses and shouted, "Here's Mrs. Sanger!"

The audience roared approval. But when she tried to speak, a priest accompanied by policemen stopped her. Challenged for their reason, the priest declared, "This meeting must be closed because an indecent, immoral subject is to be discussed."

When Margaret insisted on speaking, the policeman arrested her and marched her to a station house. Hundreds of Margaret's supporters followed them singing, "My Country, 'Tis of Thee."

Mrs. Ogden Reid, who had been in the audience, indignantly ordered an editorial in her family-owned New York *Tribune* calling the breakup of the meeting "arbitrary and Prussian to the last degree." The *Evening Post* declared, "Every liberty-loving citizen of New York is hot with indignation."

The public uproar led to a dismissal of charges in the morning. Margaret immediately rescheduled the conference. This time the publicity forced her to book the much larger Park Theater. Even then, an overflow crowd of 2,000 failed to get seats.

"I contend that it is just as sacred and beautiful for two people to express their love when they have no intention of being parents," Margaret told the audience, "and that they can go into that relationship with the same beauty and the same holiness with which they go into music or prayer."

Archbishop Hayes disagreed: "Children troop down from Heaven because God wills it. He alone has the right to stay their coming, while He blesses at will some homes with many, others with but few or with none at all. . . . To prevent human life that the Creator is about to bring into being is satanic . . . an immortal soul is denied existence in time and in eternity. It has been reserved to our day to see advocated shamelessly the legalizing of such a diabolical thing."

Margaret was denounced from pulpits as a "lascivious monster" bent on "murdering" unborn children.

In 1921, four world-famous people were invited by a major Japanese organization to lecture in Japan: Albert Einstein, Bertrand Russell, H. G. Wells, and Margaret Sanger, the only American and the only woman of the quartet.

At first, Japanese government officials put obstacles in her way, insisting that her talks on birth control would violate Japan's "Dangerous Thoughts" law. But Margaret appealed to the Imperial Diet, pointing out how birth control could reduce the dangerously overcrowded population of their tiny island. She won their consent to speak.

As a result of her lectures, a Japanese birth control committee was organized, and a Japanese edition of *Family Limitation* was published. A medical committee was organized to investigate European contraceptive practices.

Margaret also carried her message to China, which likewise had a serious problem of too many mouths to feed on a limited food supply. Droughts and floods caused millions to starve to death.

Visiting Korea, Margaret was disturbed by the subservient role women were relegated to in that society. One Korean man told her that he wanted to have twenty children, but that he now had only two. Margaret corrected him dryly: "But wasn't it your *wife* who had had the two?"

In July, 1922, she went to London to attend the first international birth control conference. That year she finally married Noah, who had been following her around the world. But she kept the name Sanger, which was by now world famous.

Margaret persuaded a young Georgia Public Health Service physician, Dr. Dorothy Bocker, to join her at the Birth Control League. Installed in two separate rooms discreetly labeled "Clinical Research Bureau," Dr. Bocker dispensed female contraceptives for "health reasons" to women directed there by Margaret. The clinic's presence was spread by word of mouth only, but that was sufficient to crowd the new birth control clinic in record time. Fully a third of the women who came were Catholic.

After two years, Dr. Bocker resigned and was replaced by Dr. Hannah Stone, whose physician husband edited the respected medical journal, *Fertility and Infertility*.

Margaret divided her time between the Birth Control League and speaking tours throughout the country and Europe. In 1924,

H. G. Wells gave an important dinner in her honor, attended by G. B. Shaw and Arnold Bennett. They encouraged her to organize the first World Population Conference in Geneva in 1927. Here scientists from many nations came together to discuss ways of restricting population to avoid world famine.

At their closing banquet, all the scientists rose to thunder a tribute to Margaret. Her exhausting work led to the creation of a permanent organization, the International Union for the Scientific Investigation of Population Problems.

Shaw called birth control "the most revolutionary idea of the century." Julian Huxley declared, "It will go down in history with the greatest advancements of the human intellect, along with the invention of the stone hammer, the mastery of fire, the discovery of electricity and the invention of printing."

Invited to Germany by a women's medical association, Margaret delivered a series of speeches which led twenty German women physicians to join birth control clinics. The German health commissioner cooperated, making his the world's first government agency to sponsor birth control.

Throughout the 1920s and 1930s, the use of contraceptives, male and female, spread at home and abroad. Catholic organizations continued to fight Margaret's appearances vigorously, trying to close halls against her.

During her frequent absences overseas, her Birth Control League came under the control of women who felt that with the movement becoming respectable, it now needed a more conservative program to win widespread acceptance. Disagreeing, Margaret angrily resigned her presidency as well as her editorship of the *Birth Control Review*.

TEN

In 1929, the police suddenly cracked down on Margaret's Clinical Research Bureau, once more for violation of the Comstock Law. A plainclothes policewoman had been fitted with a female contraceptive by Dr. Stone. She had then returned to direct police in confiscating books, contraceptive materials, and case histories of patients.

Seizure of the medical records proved a tactical police blunder. The New York County Medical Society angrily protested an obvious violation of the confidential relations between doctor and patient. A Defense Committee of Five Hundred was formed by noted American Civil Liberties Union (ACLU) lawyer Morris Ernst. It included famous ministers, doctors, lawyers, bankers, and even a former health commissioner.

At the trial, five noted doctors testified that proper spacing of births was an aid to maternal and infant health. The court ruled against the clinic, but on appeal this verdict was reversed. A furious outburst on Margaret's behalf by the press, and the indignation of the New York County Medical Society, forced Police Commissioner Grover Whalen to apologize to Margaret for the issuance of a search warrant in the first place.

"The newspapers have been wonderful to us," Margaret wrote Havelock Ellis, "and backed us 100 percent. But it put us ahead ten years, especially because of the medical testimony that from two to three years should intervene between births of children in the vast majority of cases."

The *New Yorker* now described Margaret at fifty-eight as "one of those harmless, meek-appearing little women whom wise men are wary of arousing. . . . her face in repose looks almost smiling—the expression of one who bites off nails with all the amiability in the world. . . . Her strength is an overwhelming sincerity and great personal courage."

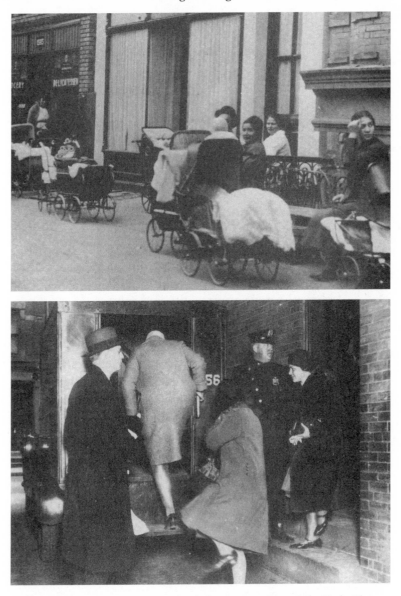

Above, Margaret Sanger's birth control clinic in Brooklyn, New York. The first to be established in the United States, it was immediately closed by the police. However, this 1929 police raid on her Clinical Research Bureau, *below*, proved a tactical blunder.

In April, 1929, Margaret became chairperson of a newly established National Committee on Federal Legislation for Birth Control. She crusaded vigorously for a federal "Doctors' Bill" that would open the mails to birth control information and devices. Travelling extensively to speak to religious organizations, she won the support of the American Unitarian Association, the Presbyterian Church, and the United Churches of Christ.

In 1930, both the US Federal Council of Churches and the Anglican Bishops of England endorsed birth control. The Pope responded with an encyclical on birth control which decreed that for Catholics only the rhythm method, based on calendar calculations of fertility days, was permissible. All other methods except abstinence were forbidden.

The American Women's Association awarded Margaret its Medal of Honor "for vision, integrity and valor . . . for fighting her battle single-handed, a pioneer of pioneers." The citation added, "She has opened the door of knowledge and given light, freedom and happiness to thousands caught in the tragic meshes of ignorance. She is remaking the world."

Congress was forced to consider Margaret's Doctors' Bill by the pressure of thousands of letters from her supporters. But the bill was blocked from Senate passage by the head of the Judiciary Committee, Senator Pat McCarran, a powerful opponent of birth control. An embittered Sanger supporter demanded that the Senate sergeant-at-arms arrest McCarran for "the murder of thousands of women!"

Disappointed by the defeat, an exhausted Margaret left for Nassau to rest and swim in the sun. Here, she wrote, she "forgot the stupidity of man and loved anew the beauties of God."

In 1935, she left for the Soviet Union to study that country's use of birth control. Margaret was disappointed to find that the USSR did little to prevent pregnancies, because of the need for a large labor force. Abortions were readily available, however, to enable women to keep working. There were few birth control clinics, and Margaret deplored their poor supplies and faulty hygiene. She was impressed, however, that most children in the Soviet Union were wanted children, and were given excellent care and schooling.

That same year, word came that Margaret's work in China was bearing fruit. The Chinese Medical Association had passed a resolution favoring birth control. Delighted, she returned to China, but landed just as Japan began its invasion of the Chinese mainland. She was forced to leave instead for India.

Here she received a great public reception and became a guest of Mahatma Gandhi. But she was disappointed by the ascetic Indian leader's refusal to endorse birth control except in the form of abstinence from marital relations.

Nevertheless, Margaret was able to persuade forty-five local East Indian medical societies to begin birth control programs. She induced fifty hospitals and clinics to set up information centers. Their problem, she learned, was convincing Indian parents whose families were too large to feed properly, but who wanted many sons to care for them in old age, that birth control would mean a better life for both parents and children.

In 1936, at long last, Margaret unexpectedly won her victory over the Comstock Law. She had ordered female contraceptives mailed from Japan to Dr. Hannah Stone at their Clinical Research Bureau. US Customs seized them. Morris Ernst of the ACLU sued the government on Margaret's behalf. The US Circuit Court of Appeals heard the case of *The United States* v. *One Package of Japanese Pessaries.* Ernst produced six noted doctors, including two former health commissioners, who testified that the birth control devices could be essential to doctors to save life or promote the well-being of patients.

The Court decided in Margaret's favor.

"Here was the culmination of unremitting labor ever since my return from Europe in 1915," Margaret wrote happily, "the gratification of seeing a dream come true."

ELEVEN

Dr. Stone wrote in *The Nation* that at last the sixty-three-year-old barrier set up by the Comstock Law was overthrown, with the birth control rights of doctors affirmed. "It established contraception as a recognized part of medical practice," she declared, "and removes the last legal barriers to the dissemination of contraceptive knowledge."

At a victory dinner given by Ernst, one of the surprise guests was the man who had been the prosecuting attorney at Margaret's *Woman Rebel* trial. He apologized publicly to her, explaining that he had only been doing his duty, but that even then he had secretly admired Margaret for her courageous crusade, just as he did now.

Dr. Robert Latou Dickinson, the eminent gynecologist, compared her to Pasteur, Florence Nightingale, and William Morton, who developed the first anesthetic. "Margaret Sanger's world-wide service holds high rank," he declared, "and is destined eventually to fullest medical recognition."

In June, 1937, the American Medical Association itself came out officially for birth control under medical supervision. Thirteen women doctors joined Margaret's Bureau staff. Physicians from all over the world flocked to the Bureau for personal instruction. Public approval of Margaret and her cause now came from the National Council of Jewish Women, the General Federation of Women's Clubs, the YWCA, and local Junior Leagues.

But Margaret had no intention of resting on her laurels. She was still searching for the perfect contraceptive, an anti-conception injection or pill that would be simple to use and readily available.

She also felt that the time was right for strengthening the birth control forces by uniting them. In 1939, she proposed a merger of her organization with the Voluntary Parenthood League. Together they became the Birth Control Federation of

America, with Margaret elected honorary president. Two years later, the BCFA became the organization known today as the Planned Parenthood Federation of America.

Margaret still had a battle on her hands in seven states which continued to outlaw the dissemination and use of contraceptives. In 1937, three Massachusetts birth control clinics were raided and closed, with records seized, and staff members arrested and fined.

Margaret started a speaking tour through that state. In Holyoke, the First Congregational Church offered to host her meeting, but felt compelled to withdraw the offer when the local Catholic church threatened to organize a boycott of Congregational-owned businesses. Margaret sought to rent other premises, but was rebuffed at every turn. Finally the Catholic head of the textile workers union, outraged at the denial of Margaret's free speech rights, offered her the use of their meeting rooms. An overflow crowd flocked to listen to her lecture.

Margaret's prestige received a tremendous boost in 1940 when the famous wife of the president, Mrs. Eleanor Roosevelt, publicly announced her support for birth control.

At another government level, however, the head of the newly created Children's Bureau of the Public Health Service, Katherine Lenroot, declared that the poverty of overlarge families was none of her business. Encouraging "biologically fit" families to have more children, she said, *was* her business. A powerful bureaucrat, Lenroot blocked Margaret's views in the Children's Bureau.

When Margaret was awarded an honorary Doctor of Laws degree from Smith College in 1949, congratulations poured in from such famous people as the Drysdales of England, China's eminent author Lin Yutang, John D. Rockefeller, Jr., and two celebrated clergymen, Raymond Fosdick and John Haynes Holmes.

After World War II, Margaret was invited to visit Japan to help that country's birth control movement. But General Douglas MacArthur, in charge of the American occupation of Japan, was pressured by Catholic Church groups to ban her from lecturing there.

"There is a problem in Japan with its tremendous yearly increase in population and its limited resources," Mrs. Roosevelt wrote in her magazine column. She added, "Mrs. Sanger was the obvious person to consult, and why our occupying forces should interfere with the wishes of the Japanese people in this respect is a little difficult to understand."

In 1951, MacArthur was relieved of his command. Margaret was then at once reinvited to Japan and accorded a tremendous welcome. Crowds mobbed her, the press lionized her, sound trucks rolled around Tokyo broadcasting, "Sanger is here! Sanger says no abortions!" In speeches, she explained that birth control would free the Japanese from the excessive population growth that had led their leaders to seek to expand their territory through disastrous wars.

The first foreigner permitted to address the Japanese Senate, Margaret persuaded the government to subsidize 53,000 midwives to teach contraception. Before she left, the birth control movement was firmly established throughout Japan.

In postwar India, she was also given an enthusiastic welcome. The government had already established two hundred birth control clinics, with one hundred more scheduled for army posts. Family planning was now the goal of a new Five-Year Plan.

A conference Margaret organized in Bombay attracted delegates from sixteen countries, as well as an American group sponsored by Mrs. Roosevelt, Albert Einstein, and other Nobel Prize winners. The conference set up the International Planned Parenthood Federation, which voted Margaret president emeritus for life.

Now quite ill, exhausted from her strenuous labors and travels, Margaret felt gratified that her work in Asia had accomplished important social changes that would survive after she had died.

Recognized around the world for her work in family planning, Margaret Sanger is interviewed by CBS's Mike Wallace.

Despite the need for frequent hospitalization, she persisted in global travels for the next eight years, seeking to make birth control a right for all women on earth. In between trips, she was active in her new home base of Tucson, Arizona, setting up a new clinic there.

She also persuaded Mrs. Kate McCormick, whose father-in-law owned International Harvester, to finance Dr. John Rock, a Catholic, in his research to develop a birth control pill. He succeeded early in the 1960s, and the pill revolutionized the science of planned parenthood.

TWELVE

Margaret was also influential in persuading the Ford Foundation to provide a million dollars for a worldwide study on population control.

In 1959, when Margaret was eighty, she made a farewell tour of Japan and India. She felt vindicated when the grateful government of Japan revealed to her that the island's birthrate had been reduced by more than half, thanks to the family planning programs she had introduced.

In India, she attended the Sixth International Family Planning Conference in New Delhi, where she was escorted to the platform by Prime Minister Jawaharlal Nehru.

The assembly passed a resolution which declared, "Through her indomitable courage, her steadfast dedication and her great vision for nearly half a century, Margaret Sanger has seen her mission come to fruition in the development of national organizations united in the International Federation, and the governmental acceptance of family planning in several countries. The 750 delegates and observers from twenty-seven countries assembled . . . offer to Margaret Sanger their deep admiration, affection and gratitude."

In 1961, Sir Julian Huxley organized a World Tribute luncheon at which $100,000 was donated for the continuation of her work. At another dinner in her honor she was presented with a medal from the Emperor of Japan, which she enjoyed wearing over her nightgown upon retiring.

By 1962, utterly worn out, feeble, and seriously ill, the woman who had devoted her life to the care of the world's mothers had to be cared for herself in a nursing home.

In her last years, she had the satisfaction of knowing that her cause, once considered unmentionable and shocking, had become respectable around the world. Pearl Buck said, "No cause ever fought has been fought against more stupid, blind social prejudice, not even the cause of the people against the divine right of kings, nor the cause of equal suffrage, nor any of the battles of freedom."

Although the Catholic Church remained officially opposed to birth control other than the rhythm method, polls showed that the vast majority of American Catholic families were using contraceptives. And it was Catholic lawyers who overturned a Connecticut statute against birth control clinics by winning a verdict that the law violated married couples' right to privacy under the Fourteenth Amendment.

In 1966, a thousand admirers gathered in Tucson to pay honor to Margaret as she lay dying in the nursing home. The US Department of Health, Education, and Welfare announced a series of regional conferences to assist states and communities in developing and expanding birth control programs—an ironic about-face from the days when the government persecuted Margaret Sanger for doing the same thing.

Margaret never knew of this final vindication because she lay in a coma, dying of arteriosclerosis the next day, September 6, 1966, at age eighty-seven. Funeral tributes came from all over the world to the woman who had helped hundreds of millions of mothers around the world to have wanted children, spaced for the best health of mother and child, and for the happiness and welfare of the whole family.

Margaret Sanger's accomplishment becomes even more important in light of demographers' warnings that without intensified world birth control, the earth's population could double in the next century, creating hunger and misery for hundreds of millions of families. Should the world manage to solve this grave problem, it will be thanks to Margaret for having pointed the way.

If Margaret was a fanatic, she was a courageous fanatic who persisted in struggling against overwhelming odds on behalf of women everywhere, in a battle that only the determined dedication of a fanatic could win.

Betty Friedan

1921–2006

"Liberation now! Equality now!"

ONE

There had never been anything like it. More than 2,000 years after Aristophanes' comic play *Lysistrata* first raised the possibility of a women's strike, the women of America were making it a reality. Though the women in the play went on strike against sleeping with their husbands as a way to end their war, this strike in 1970 was a protest against oppressive male-imposed conditions.

The strike was chiefly the work of Mrs. Betty Friedan. Then the world's leading spokesperson for women's rights, she was determined to demonstrate the power of the modern women's movement. Strike demands included equal opportunity in employment and education, the legalization of abortion, and twenty-four-hour child-care centers for working women.

The event was scheduled for a weekday afternoon, August 26, the fiftieth anniversary of the Nineteenth Amendment giving American women the right to vote. While that amendment was being debated in 1920, suffragettes, bearing a petition signed by over a million women, had marched in a huge parade down Fifth Avenue in New York City to demand the vote. Betty planned to dramatize the 1970 strike by organizing another enormous parade down Fifth Avenue to demand sweeping social changes in America for women.

The organization she had founded, the National Organization for Women (NOW), solicited and won support for similar town and city marches and demonstrations across the nation. Betty asked secretaries to put covers on their typewriters, telephone operators to unplug their switchboards, waitresses to stop serving meals, cleaning women to put up their mops, and wives to stop cooking and making love that night.

Many different moderate and radical women's groups turned out for the parade, as well as housewives, secretaries, professionals, students, suburbanites, factory workers, and some seventy- and eighty-year-old veterans of the suffragette movement. They marched behind challenging signs declaring:

REPENT, MALE CHAUVINISTS,
YOUR WORLD IS COMING TO AN END!

OPPRESSED WOMEN:
DON'T COOK DINNER!
STARVE A RAT TODAY!

I LOVE YOU, SUSAN ANTHONY

LYSISTRATA RIDES AGAIN!

Journalist Gloria Steinem carried a sign showing a picture of a child victim of the My Lai massacre in the Vietnam War. Its ironic caption, a takeoff of Betty Friedan's book, *The Feminine Mystique*, read: the masculine mystique.

The House of Representatives, alarmed by the spectre of an uprising of American women voters, hastily dusted off the long-buried Equal Rights Amendment (ERA), and passed it just before the march took place. The Senate also vowed to pass it, but when the excitement died down after the march, this promise was quietly forgotten.

Impressed by the growing women's liberation movement, President Richard Nixon issued a proclamation reminding all Americans to "recognize the great debt we owe" to the suffragettes, and pledging a "wider role" for women in all walks of life. The Post Office Department lost no time issuing a stamp commemorating the suffragettes' fiftieth anniversary.

New York governor Nelson D. Rockefeller proclaimed August 26 a holiday. In his speech, he praised three outstanding fighters for women's rights: Susan B. Anthony, Elizabeth Cady Stanton, and Betty Friedan.

But suddenly preparations for the march were threatened. New York mayor John Lindsay refused to issue a permit for the women to march down Fifth Avenue. He explained that they would create a terrible traffic jam. Besides, Fifth Avenue businesses would suffer!

Betty and her parade organizers were outraged. Irish, Italian, and other ethnic groups were regularly allowed to use Fifth Avenue for their parades. For the St. Patrick's Day parade, a green stripe was even painted down the avenue. And fifty years earlier, the suffragettes had been allowed to parade there. Why, then, were the feminists of 1970 being discriminated against?

Reporters besieged Betty. Was she calling off NOW's parade? Or would she have to hold the march on the sidewalks of Fifth Avenue? No, she replied, the parade would take place as scheduled. "I don't believe," she declared, "the mayor will persist in this insult to women."

But Lindsay refused to lift the ban and discreetly fled to Jackson Hole in Wyoming. Women wondered whether they would have to fight their way down the avenue through squads of mounted police armed with clubs and tear gas, and face arrest for violating a city ordinance.

When Betty left strike headquarters for the parade assembly point at the entrance to Central Park on 59th Street, she was astonished at the size of the crowd she found. Over 25,000 people had gathered for the parade, among them hundreds of sympathetic men marching with wives and girlfriends.

Some celebrated faces stood out in the crowd: suffragette Judge Dorothy Kenyon, editor Helen Gurley Brown, journalist Shana Alexander, author Kate Millett, and Eleanor Holmes Norton, chairperson of the NY Commission on Human Rights.

The sun was shining for the demonstration, which marked the largest single protest against woman's inequality in American history. One NOW official declared enthusiastically, "God has blessed us in the movement with a beautiful day—hasn't She?"

When Betty led the march onto Fifth Avenue, the women were confronted by a large number of mounted police who tried to press them off the street and onto the sidewalks. But the police quickly realized that the parade was too large to move off the avenue. They then attempted to confine it to only one lane.

But Betty took the hands of the women on either side of her and shouted in her husky voice, "Take hands and stretch across the whole street!" All the women in the first rank quickly fanned out, while the word passed to the ranks behind. The women surged downtown across the full width of the avenue, pressing the baffled mounted police back to the sidelines.

Fifth Avenue buses and cars ground to a halt in a huge traffic jam. The blare of their horns was drowned out by women shouting Betty's slogan: "Liberation Now! Equality Now!" North of 60th Street, Fifth Avenue was a sea of cars; south of it a sea of marching women.

"Why don't you girls get married?" shouted a male heckler.

A young black woman raised the arms of two sons marching with her and shouted back, "I'm married and I'm here!"

When the march reached Bryant Park, speakers addressed the huge crowd. Betty Friedan delivered the major address.

"We have learned," she declared, "that the enemy is us—our own lack of self-confidence. We now know that the enemy is not men—there were men marching with us today, men who can say, 'We don't have to be dominant and superior to everybody in the world to prove our manhood.'. . . In the orthodox religion of my ancestors, every day is begun with the prayer, Thank Thee, Lord, that I was not born a woman.'" She took a deep breath.

"Today," she went on, "I feel absolutely sure that every woman in the world will say, Thank Thee, Lord, that I *was* born a woman!'" The audience roared approval in a prolonged ovation.

Recording the event later, Betty wrote, "Many reporters, male, wrote afterward that they'd never seen so many beautiful women as the proud and joyous crowd who marched down Fifth Avenue that day."

After the August 26th strike, which was extensively covered by the media, one survey found that four out of five American adults had "read or heard about women's liberation."

And the principal reason that they had was Betty Friedan.

TWO

She was born Betty Goldstein in Peoria, Illinois, on February 4, 1921, the first of three children. Her father, Harry, was a Jewish immigrant from Eastern Europe who had come to America as a child. Her mother, Miriam Horwitz, was born in Peoria but also of East European parents. Both of Betty's parents were great influences in her life.

Her mother was a woman of great ability and energy who loved working as editor of the woman's page of their local newspaper. But after she married Harry, she had to give up the job because it was customary for middle-class married women of that day to stay home as housewives. Beautifully dressed, Miriam Goldstein served on the Community Chest, played bridge and mah-jongg, ran the Hadassah Sunday School, played golf and tennis, and was a superb hostess and decorator. But these activities did not offer Betty's mother sufficient outlet for her talents and vitality, and she was discontented with her life.

"When I was little and said prayers before I went to sleep," Betty told me, "I put in a couple of wishes. I wanted a boy to like me best, and I wanted to find some work to do that would use my energy. I could see that that was what was wrong with my mother."

Her mother transferred her frustrated ambitions to making excessive demands on her husband and children, and to extravagant shopping for unessential purchases. Her spending sprees led to frequent battles with her husband.

Betty was the apple of her proud father's eye. Extremely bright, she earned top marks at school and skipped two grades. Her father treasured everything she wrote so much that he kept it all in his safe. Although Betty suspected that he would have preferred that she had been a son, he never said so.

In another era, Betty would probably have been groomed for Harvard Law School, like all of her boy cousins, but in that era Harvard Law didn't admit women.

She was determined not to grow up to lead an empty life like her mother's. Nor did Miriam Goldstein want the daughter she loved to grow up settling as she had for an existence in the shadow of a husband. When Betty entered junior high, her mother urged her to write for the school paper. In high school, she encouraged Betty to start and edit a literary magazine.

Living vicariously through her daughter's literary successes, Miriam Goldstein could hardly wait for Betty to enter college and become editor of its newspaper.

Blessed with a vivid imagination as a child, Betty discovered that she was very good at organizing groups and inventing games. She was always starting clubs in the family basement. Soon after organizing one club, Betty would grow bored with it, and go on to organize something new. This pattern foreshadowed her talents as an organizer in school, college, and adult life. She often provided the original vision and impetus for a club or project, would get it organized, then move on to bring new visions to life.

Mischievous as a child, Betty had no use for "mealy-mouthed, do-good types." She organized a "Baddy Baddy Club" to make life miserable for a substitute teacher she couldn't stand. When Betty gave the cue, the club members would have loud coughing fits, or let their books fall to the floor with a resonant bang. But the principal recognized Betty as the ringleader, and chastened her into disbanding the Baddy Baddy Club.

To channel some of her boundless energy, Betty joined a neighborhood children's theater, writing skits for homeroom programs, and acting in them as well. Although her mother insisted that Betty take music lessons, she showed no musical aptitude. Her mother allowed her to switch to dramatic lessons instead. She loved being in plays, and in high school won a dramatic prize for portraying the madwoman in *Jane Eyre*.

"I would probably have had the ambition to be an actress," Betty told me, "except that an actress, in the era before Barbra Streisand, had to be conventionally pretty. When I went to college I stopped acting because I became editor of the Smith paper, and editor of a literary magazine I started. However, I'm still able to use my dramatic ability today because one of the ways I make my living is to lecture, and I'm a very good lecturer."

Betty was appalled when she encountered anti-Semitism in high school. In the sororities which dominated student social life in the Midwest, it was an unspoken fact of life. All the Christian girls from Betty's class in grade school were admitted to the sororities, but Betty, along with every other Jewish girl, was not.

Feeling terribly isolated, she assuaged her loneliness with stacks of books from the library. She loved to read, devouring books at the rate of one or two a day. As a young child, she had belonged to the Literary Guild Children's Book Club. By the time she was six she had outgrown *The Bobbsey Twins,* and was soon reading *Little Women,* stories by Willa Cather, and plays by John Galsworthy.

When she ventured out to a high school dance, Betty felt at a disadvantage because she was younger than her classmates, still wearing "Mary Janes"—children's shoes with rounded toes and a strap. Besides, she was less attractive than most, and a clumsy dancer. For a couple of years, she was friendless until she gradually made new friends who shared her interest in journalism.

"I had a miserable adolescence," Betty told me, "certainly not unique to me. More people than you realize have a miserable adolescence. And I spent more time reading poetry on grave-stones than I really wanted to do. No Emily Dickinson, I!"

If her social life was lacking, she loved the academic side of school. She enjoyed the challenge of tests, and had excellent teachers both in grammar school and high school. With a flair for chemistry, Betty at one time dreamed of becoming a famous chemist. But her chemistry teacher scoffed, "Who do you think you are—a future Marie Curie?" The teacher told Betty that women could not expect careers as scientists.

THREE

When Betty left for Smith College in the East, her father advised her not to return to Peoria after college because there was no scope for her ability there. Since Betty was very bright, he believed she needed to thrive in a brighter world.

She found Smith enormously challenging and exciting. Its atmosphere of social concern and social responsibility influenced her greatly. Becoming editor of the college paper, she was thrilled to be able to interview one of the great ladies of the century, Mrs. Eleanor Roosevelt.

While Betty was a whiz at math, she was helpless at physics. She made a pact with some football players in a nearby college to do their work in math if they did her experiments in physics. The football team turned out to cheer Betty when she became valedictorian of her graduating class.

Having grown up in parochial Peoria, she had never read newspapers until she reached Smith. In college during the early forties, her horizons were widened as she learned about Socialism, Communism, and Fascism, and saw their forces at work in the Spanish Civil War, the incubator of World War II. She was fascinated by the book *Middletown* by Robert and Helen Lynd, because it psychoanalyzed the kind of town in which she had grown up.

During the summer of 1940, her economics professor encouraged nineteen-year-old Betty to assist a writers' conference at the Highlander Folk School in Tennessee. Highlander was an unusual place which had spawned early labor organizing, and which would later be the birthplace of the civil rights anthem, "We Shall Overcome."

Here Betty developed both her writing and her social conscience. She became passionate about social justice, the inequities of the Depression, and the rights of workers. Like most intellectuals of that time, Betty romanticized socialism as a better system than capitalism.

She started the *Smith College Monthly,* a literary magazine, which served as a showcase for many of her short stories, poems, and essays. She was now sufficiently aware of international affairs to warn that if Hitler, who had begun overrunning Europe, were not stopped, fascism could come to America as well.

In her junior year, Betty became editor-in-chief of the Smith College newspaper, *SCAN,* with a staff of eighty girls. When she tried to expose a snobbish secret sorority of wealthy girls, the college president threatened to expel the reporters who had dug up the story. Betty ran a page in the next issue blank except for the word, "CENSORED," not unlike the ploy the *Socialist Call* had used when Comstock had banned Margaret Sanger's article.

When Betty graduated from Smith summa cum laude, she was awarded a fellowship for graduate study in psychology at Berkeley. After winning her master's degree there, she was offered another fellowship leading to a PhD. But Betty turned it down because America was now at war, and she felt a strong need to do something for the war effort against world fascism.

She volunteered for Red Cross work overseas, but was rejected because she had developed severe asthma at Smith. She was, besides, under the required minimum age of twenty-five.

Leaving Berkeley in 1943, Betty moved to New York, where she shared a Greenwich Village apartment with some Smith classmates. Her father's foresight was validated as Betty found herself enormously stimulated by life in a community of writers, journalists, academics, and people involved in the arts.

She sought a newspaper job that would provide scope for her social conscience. Applying at Federated Press, she was asked if she knew the difference between the AFL and the CIO "I wasn't sure," Betty recalls, "but I said I knew that one of them was more radical than the other. From that they figured that I wasn't a Communist, so they hired me."

She suddenly found herself plunged into the rough-and-tumble real world, covering a number of strikes, including one bitter Philadelphia transit strike against racial prejudice. She covered the first International Labor Conference after the war, and interviewed Eleanor Roosevelt once again.

Because she was a woman on a not very large staff, Betty was given a recipe column to write. "I didn't cook," she chuckles, "so I was always putting down half a cup of salt when it should have been half a teaspoon. There was great criticism of the recipes in my column, but I would always figure out ingenious ways of explaining the discrepancies."

At Federated Press, she learned to get the real story by looking beneath surface appearances and the official story to the "grubby economic underside of American reality." When electric plant workers, who were mostly women, went out on strike, Betty learned and reported that they were not only being dealt with unfairly by management, but also by their own union.

She had to give up her job when a war veteran returned to claim the place she had filled. Returning veterans made jobs for women scarce after the war. Betty applied for work as a *Time-Life* researcher, even though she knew that women researchers were never promoted to writers or editors. When that didn't pan out, she found a job on a labor union paper for electrical workers.

Through her many interviews with workers, she gained insight into what everyday life was really like for working men and women. She quickly learned that women were not paid as much as men who did the same work. Betty wrote a pamphlet for the union showing how unfair treatment of women let companies hold down men's pay as well.

By this time, she was living in her own apartment. One day, she was visited by a returning veteran, Carl Friedan, a friend of one of Betty's fellow reporters. Made desperate by a New York apartment shortage, Carl brought Betty an apple, made her laugh at his jokes, and persuaded her to let him move in.

He was fascinated by her inexhaustible energy and enthusiasm. When they talked, she was constantly breaking off one sentence to begin another, her bright mind racing so fast that her words couldn't keep up. Carl was soon in love.

They were married in 1947 when Betty was twenty-six. Carl ran a summer theater and served as a barely paid editor of a theatrical magazine. After baby Daniel was born, Betty took a maternity leave from her job to stay home and nurse him. Then, paying for child care, she went back to work. But she was fired soon afterward in 1949 for becoming pregnant again, and a man was hired to replace her.

Betty's union contract allowed for maternity leaves, but her appeal to the union went unheeded. She was told that getting pregnant a second time was a "personal matter," her own "fault," not anything a union could fight for on her behalf. Not until years later, when the term came into common use, did she perceive her firing as a matter of sex discrimination.

FOUR

"After I was fired our finances became very perilous," Betty told me, "so Carl left the summer theater for regular paychecks in advertising and public relations." She augmented their income by writing articles for popular magazines. "I got top article rates, but I couldn't find the time to write more than five or six articles a year. I didn't earn a lot of money, but what I did earn was necessary for our standard of living."

Betty and Carl were troubled when Senator Joseph McCarthy held his infamous hearings, creating a phony Red scare in America. To fight against such bigotry and illiberalism, Betty became editor of a small community newspaper.

In 1948, when she was eight months pregnant, she mounted a stepladder to give a street speech for progressive Henry Wallace's presidential campaign. But a year later, she became less concerned with politics, and more interested in houses and furnishings.

She and Carl moved into a new garden apartment community in Queens called Parkway Village after Betty read that it had a fine cooperative nursery school. Here she settled down to a life of domesticity, as so many housewives did in 1949, following the urgings of the women's magazines to seek fulfillment as housewives and mothers, not as career women.

Raising three children, Betty socialized with other neighborhood stay-at-home mothers, both college graduates and women without higher education, all of whom seemed to be living exclusively for the blessings of home and child rearing in accordance with media brainwashing. At the time, Betty had no name for this idealized vision of a woman's proper lifestyle. Only later was she to identify it as the "Feminine Mystique."

She and Carl subsequently bought a fine old Victorian house on the Hudson River in Rockland County, New York.

"It seemed like we were working to support this house," Betty recalled. "It took every penny we had."

In 1953, Frenchwoman Simone de Beauvoir created an international stir with her book, *The Second Sex*. It accused the world's patriarchal societies of still treating women as second-class citizens. "Man is defined as a human being and woman as a female," de Beauvoir protested. "Whenever she behaves as a human being she is said to imitate the male."

Betty, meanwhile, was becoming irked and bored writing the type of articles that women's magazine editors demanded, with the subjects strictly limited to romance, marriage, home decoration, food, pregnancy, child care, and health. It was as though, Betty fretted, the whole wide world that both men and women lived and worked in didn't exist.

In 1956, she attended a Smith College reunion, an event that was to change her life. As a former editor of the college paper and magazine, and a summa cum laude graduate in psychology, Betty was asked to prepare a candid questionnaire for two hundred of her alumnae classmates. The purpose was to see what use they had made of their Smith education in the fifteen years since graduation, and how they felt about their life experiences.

Sensing that the study could make an interesting magazine article, Betty spent a full year exploring the concept in depth. It would prove, she believed, that a good education did not prevent women from adjusting to happy lives as housewives.

But when Betty studied all the answers to the questionnaires, many of them written with great detail, she was startled to discover that her premise was totally wrong. The responses revealed that the women identified themselves only as a husband's wife, their children's mother, a full-time housewife, or a glorified sex object. They had no sense of themselves as individuals.

Trying to live up to the roles society had assigned them had not made them happy. They weren't sure why, and most blamed their discontent on themselves, feeling guiltily that something must be wrong with them. Each woman imagined that she was alone and unique in her dissatisfaction with living primarily for and through her husband and children.

Betty began to recognize in these admissions the same syndrome in herself. She sensed that something was wrong with trying to fit into the stunted mold society had allotted women. In effect, they were living a lie, not being true to their own real desires and aspirations. Betty concluded that the American culture did not permit women to acknowledge and satisfy their need to grow and fulfill their potential as human beings.

In significant contrast, men never defined themselves as husbands or fathers or householders, but almost always in terms of their work or careers.

Most women, Betty found, had been directed to college as the place to find a man, not to stretch their minds and gain the education and training that would allow them to enter a career at a meaningful level.

Of the two hundred women who answered Betty's questionnaire, 89 percent had become housewives. They regretted that they had not taken their education at Smith seriously enough to put it to important use. Six out of ten did not feel fulfilled as housewives, and did not enjoy housework.

When Betty had concluded her research, she received an assignment from *McCall's* to write an article reporting her findings. But when the male editors read her article, they rejected it emphatically, declaring that Betty's picture of what life was really like for most women couldn't be true. She suspected that the real reason was that the image of happy female domesticity pleased magazine advertisers, presumably putting women readers in a docile mood conducive to buying more products for the home.

To analyze and strengthen her research, Betty personally interviewed many more women of all ages, including psychologists, editors, sociologists, family life experts, and marriage counselors. When her article was next offered to the *Ladies' Home Journal,* to Betty's chagrin the editors accepted it only to rewrite it to prove the exact opposite of what her research showed. Although she could well have used the several thousand dollars it would have paid her, Betty withdrew the article.

Her agent then offered it to *Redbook,* whose editor promptly rejected it. The editor told the agent that Betty was crazy to think that any reader except "the most neurotic housewife" could identify with the women in her survey.

Exasperated, Betty told her agent that apparently the only way she was going to be able to get her findings published was by writing a book. The agent procured a thousand dollar advance for such a book from W.W. Norton & Company. Betty thought it would take her a year to write. It took five years.

FIVE

She spent two years writing it at a rent-free desk in the New York Public Library, taking a bus into the city three days a week. For the next three years she continued writing it on her dining room table, living room couch, and on a dock by a river.

Until this time, Betty had not been particularly interested in women's problems. But she felt compelled to write her book because the articles she herself, and others, had been writing for the women's magazines now seemed based on false assumptions. At the same time, she realized that she was living her own personal life in lockstep with these assumptions, just like the other discontented women in her research.

At first, Betty thought of her subject as "The Problem That Has No Name." But her library studies of the way women were presented in women's magazines during the 1950s and early 1960s led her to define the problem as "the Feminine Mystique." This was a belief system that women had accepted and modeled their lives after, only to find that it had not brought them the happiness and fulfillment it promised. Magazines in the "happy housewife" era contained no hint of the silent dissatisfaction felt by millions of women.

Betty found that women's magazines of the 1930s and 1940s, in contrast, had published hundreds of articles on the same broad range of subjects that appeared in magazines read by men. Many of the women cast as role models in those pages, in both fiction and articles, were portrayed as dynamic career women who defined themselves by their place in the world, not by their family lives. This trend was accentuated during World War II, when women were encouraged to replace soldiers in the work force.

But this publishing era had been succeeded by magazines whose pages featured heroines who gave up their careers, stepping aside for returning veterans when they "realized" that what they really wanted was to "fulfill their femininity" as housewives. The media was then obviously attempting to discourage women from pursuing careers by praising their roles as housewives and mothers. By now, Betty felt certain that behind the campaign was the desire of advertisers, who had to switch from marketing the war effort to marketing consumer goods, to make big profits selling more washing machines, dryers, freezers, food products, and home appliances.

Men bought the Feminine Mystique as well as women. Even Adlai Stevenson, the liberal Democratic candidate for president in 1952 and 1956, declared that the ideal role for educated women in politics was not to participate themselves, but to influence the men who did.

As Betty worked on her book, analyzing and rethinking her research and her interviews, she began to realize that her own life was changing. Her work was raising her own consciousness about the difference between the programmed life she had been leading, and the freer, unstructured life she needed.

"We can no longer ignore," Betty concluded, "that voice within women that says: 'I want something more than my husband and my children and my home.'"

She concealed the fact that she was writing her book from her neighbors, aware that it might upset many housewives who were victims of the Feminine Mystique. It might also confuse wives forced to work outside the home to help their husbands pay bills, but who felt guilty for not staying home to look after their children. In 1960, women made up a third of the nation's work force, usually in low-status, low-paying jobs.

Betty learned that each woman felt alone in her dilemma, thinking herself something of a freak for not adjusting well to the Feminine Mystique. In her book, Betty urged women to face the problem honestly, asking themselves, "What do I really want to do?" When they did that, they could begin to find their own answers, ways in which they could change their lives to improve their own self-image, rather than trying to live up to someone else's ideal of wife, mother, or homemaker.

To get out of her trap, Betty declared, a woman needed higher education and professional training, so she could develop creative work of her own. With lifetime interests and goals to pursue, women would also be fully occupied after the child-rearing years, thus avoiding emotional bankruptcy when their children left home. Betty called for a national educational program for women, similar to the GI Bill that had made higher education possible for returning war veterans.

She also wanted educators, parents, and clergy to warn against early marriages, as these often curtailed higher education. Teenage girls, Betty wrote, should also be taught that they could aspire to higher and more fulfilling goals than becoming "just a housewife." Toward that end, women needed to agitate for maternity leave and child-care agencies. Then they could pursue careers on an equal level with men, without having to sacrifice either marriage or motherhood.

Betty warned that defying the Feminine Mystique would take courage. Women would have to face the envy, hostility, and resentment of other housewives who lived vicariously through their husbands and children, and who could not or would not seek lives of their own.

Published in 1967, *The Feminine Mystique* hit the nation like a bombshell.

SIX

Reviews and word of mouth made the book an instant sensation and bestseller. At one stroke, Betty exploded the simplistic myth of women as happy little homemakers. Arguments raged over Betty's insistence that women were intensely dissatisfied with their second-class citizenship, with subordinating their own need for growth and development to the needs of husbands, and with their lack of equal opportunity in the marketplace.

Women began to think about Betty's charge that those who were unhappy with the lives they were forced to lead were labeled misfits and neurotics, made to feel guilty about their dissatisfaction.

"I didn't blame women for being scared," Betty wrote later. "I was pretty scared myself. It isn't really possible to make a new pattern of life all by yourself."

Across the country, cocktail parties broke up over angry arguments about her book. Outraged letters from housewives denounced Betty as a destroyer of the family, an enemy of motherhood, a betrayal of femininity. The book was also attacked by such celebrities as anthropologist Margaret Mead, author Midge Decter, and conservative spokeswoman Phyllis Schlafly.

Betty and Carl were suddenly dropped from the guest lists for neighborhood dinner parties. Their children were rejected from the car pool, excluded from art and dancing classes. Ostracized in the suburbs, the Friedans were forced to move back to the city.

At the same time, thousands of letters poured in to Betty from suburban housewives who were thrilled with her book, validating her findings with their own experiences. Many expressed relief at discovering that they were not alone in trying to move in society "not just as my husband's wife, my children's mother, but as myself."

Speaking engagements at home and abroad brought Betty before large audiences of women who voiced their own dissatisfaction. For millions of housewives and female workers, her book had put into words what they had long secretly felt, but had been afraid to face or express.

The book was soon translated into thirteen languages. Many women credited *The Feminine Mystique* with changing their lives. Betty found that it had changed her own life, too. In the eye of the feminist storm she had unleashed, she became fired with the desire to do more than just give voice to women's grievances. She made it her lifelong goal to end them.

Travelling constantly, she listened as well as lectured to more and more women, urging them to break the chains of passivity that bound them. Sparked by Betty's book, the women's liberation movement began to grow steadily.

Emboldened by her own words, Betty forced herself to face an intense fear of flying which had handicapped her travels. She overcame it by flying to all her speaking engagements and conferences across the US and around the world, in everything from airliners to single-engine cloud hoppers.

With *The Feminine Mystique* a hot best-seller, the very magazines that had earlier rejected Betty's articles on the subject now rushed to publish excerpts from the book. Excerpts in *McCall's* brought such a storm of letters from readers that the editor urged Betty to write an article analyzing the letters.

In 1964, editor Clay Felker of the *Ladies' Home Journal* asked her to lunch at the Oak Room of the Plaza Hotel. She arrived before he did, and when she went to wait for him at the bar, she was told that unescorted women were not allowed. When she asked instead to wait for Felker in the Oak Room, she was informed that women could not be served lunch there. Her luncheon appointment was switched to another room in the Plaza.

Indignant at being discriminated against because she was a woman, Betty took her revenge four years later. She and members of the National Organization for Women (NOW) staged a sit-in protest at the Plaza's Oak Room, as part of national demonstrations against segregated eating places. Soon afterward, New York, Pennsylvania, and other states passed laws banning sex discrimination in public accommodations.

Impressed by the national stir over *The Feminine Mystique,* the *Ladies' Home Journal* offered to turn over a complete issue to Betty to guest-edit. After she was persuaded to take the assignment, male editors rejected one of her articles dealing with women and money, as well as every short story Betty wanted to include. The editors considered the stories too inflammatory, for they showed women as they really were, and not as *The Feminine Mystique* wanted them to be.

Despite this censorship, Betty's issue evoked a storm of controversy from the *Journal's* five million readers. The editor-in-chief was fired. The magazine then apologized to its offended readers by rapidly throwing together an antifeminist issue, reestablishing the "traditional values" of women as housewife-consumers.

Betty's scathing criticism of the women's media led Gloria Steinem to found the first feminist magazine six years later. Steinem was a young journalist who created a sensation by taking a job as a "bunny" in a Playboy club for men, and exposing these clubs for exploiting and demeaning women for male titillation. Convinced that no American magazine really reflected the views of modern, independent women, or spoke to them honestly, Steinem launched *Ms.,* which quickly achieved national influence.

TV Guide asked Betty to analyze how women were being portrayed in TV programs. After watching two weeks of soap operas, sitcoms, game shows, and commercials, she wrote a sizzling two-part attack on television's sexist image of women. Readers who felt insulted by their image on TV flooded *TV Guide* with mail, the greatest response they had ever received for an article.

Women's liberation stirred congresswomen to put pressure on their male colleagues. In 1964, Congress felt compelled to add an article to the Civil Rights Act banning sex discrimination as well as race discrimination in employment.

The Feminine Mystique brought the distorted image of women in the media into close focus, igniting a wave of protest. At *right*, feminist Ann Simonton wears a gown of cold cuts to protest the 1982 Miss California Pageant as a female "meat market." *Below*, a poster carried during the 1971 New York City march questions women's portrayal in advertising.

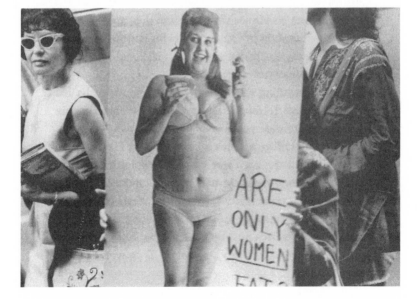

"Who cares?" shrugged one senator. "How is any woman going to prove that she was discriminated against in a job just because she's a woman?" It soon proved, indeed, that the government had no serious intention of enforcing the law, but was simply paying lip service to the fight against sex discrimination.

Betty began commuting to Washington to research a second book she was writing. Studying federal agencies, she found widespread sex discrimination in all of them. Only a token woman here and there was promoted, and then only as a minor official.

Even though the law now prohibited newspapers from running sex-segregated help-wanted ads, "Help Wanted Male" ads for the good jobs still appeared separately from "Help Wanted Female" ads for the low-paying jobs. The Equal Employment Opportunity Commission (EEOC) made no attempt to enforce compliance with the law.

Sonia Pressman, a young woman lawyer for the EEOC, met secretly with Betty to urge her to initiate an independent women's organization to fight for women's rights, the way the NAACP fought for black rights. Betty, by now convinced that writing and speaking were not enough to effect change, decided to turn to direct action.

State commissioners on the status of women had gathered in Washington for a national conference. Betty invited fifteen of the women to meet informally in her hotel room. She proposed that they join in starting a feminist organization to fight for equality. At first, the women commissioners refused. But they became outraged when the Johnson administration made a mockery of their hearings by bluntly telling them they had no power to take any action at all, or even to offer a resolution.

The angry women phoned Betty and now agreed to her proposal. Meeting at a hotel in June, 1966, they organized the National Organization for Women (NOW).

SEVEN

Betty wrote NOW's purpose on a paper napkin: "To take the actions needed to bring women into the mainstream of American society, now; full equality for women, in fully equal partnership with men." She was helped to get the organization under way by Congresswoman Martha Griffiths of Michigan, who had been prevented from raising feminist issues before an EEOC hearing.

NOW was founded officially on October 29, 1966, and Betty was elected president. She lost no time in charging that women were denied decent jobs and wages, black women especially. Companies would not be able to escape NOW's criticism by hiring a "token" woman executive. And NOW intended to fight the deliberate barring of women from postgraduate education and professional associations.

NOW rapidly became a powerful organization advancing the rights of American women. It was also largely responsible for getting Congress to pass the Equal Rights Amendment, fought by conservatives led by Phyllis Schlafly, head of the Eagle Forum. The ERA failed to become part of the Constitution, however, because by June 30, 1982, after a sixty-year battle, only thirty-five states had ratified the amendment, three short of the thirty-eight needed.

In one interview, Betty vowed that NOW would use every available political tactic to end sex discrimination. "We don't even exclude the possibility," she warned, "of a mass march on Washington." Said one of NOW's three hundred charter members, "NOW scared the wits out of the government."

NOW became the first militant feminist group in the twentieth century to combat sex discrimination in every sphere of life. Wherever Betty spoke around the country, she left behind another new enthusiastic chapter of NOW.

Betty was reelected NOW's president for the next three years. But because the post paid nothing, she continued to support her family through book royalties, article sales, and lecture fees, in equal share with Carl. When she finally stepped down as NOW's president, she began accepting teaching posts at various universities.

NOW's struggle to unify women in the feminist movement was not an easy one. Many women feared offending husbands, fathers, and male bosses. They were also divided by their roles as wives, mothers, workers, and career women, as well as by class, race, religion, and ethnic background. NOW was also handicapped by the ridicule of the male-controlled media. Many women were frightened off by media portrayals of feminists as strident viragos and man-hating lesbians. Enemies of the women's liberation movement referred contemptuously to it as "Women's Lib," and to its practitioners as "women's libbers."

But nothing daunted Betty. She worked tirelessly night and day to make NOW powerful enough to force Congress and the White House to take women's issues seriously. NOW finally compelled employers to stop running separate want ads for men and women, making all jobs open to both sexes.

NOW also went after companies that barred women from applying for jobs traditionally held by men. Heavy industries, railroad, trucking, and construction companies as well as firefighting companies, sought to bar the employment of women with legislation "protecting" women from having to lift over thirty-five pounds. NOW fought the law as discriminatory, and won.

NOW also went after companies that committed age as well as sex discrimination, firing older women to save the cost of pensions and promotions, then replacing them with lower-salaried younger women.

Betty led a delegation that pressed the EEOC to explain why it had no woman lawyer as a major executive in its own agency, which was supposed to fight discrimination. A male commissioner hastily explained that he was interviewing "girls" to fill one

Betty Friedan

Betty Friedan speaks at the women's rights march of August 26, 1971. The signs of the protesters, *below*, reflect the diverse issues the march addressed.

opening. He couldn't understand why the delegation laughed, until Betty dryly informed him that calling lawyers "girls" was patronizing. The confused commissioner tried "ladies." That drew more derisive laughter as Betty sighed an explanation that "women" was the correct appellation.

On Christmas Eve, 1966, Betty was subpoenaed to testify in a federal court as a result of NOW's charge that the airlines were guilty of sex discrimination. Stewardesses were being forced to quit when they married or reached age thirty. The airlines demanded that Betty provide a list of NOW's members. She refused, knowing that stewardesses who were found to be members would be fired as "troublemakers." The EEOC finally had to take action and stop the airlines' sex discrimination.

On Betty's subsequent flights, she found herself hugged by over-thirty stewardesses, many of whom were married and even had children.

On Mother's Day in 1967, she organized a picket line at the White House fence. Women on the line demanded "Rights, Not Roses" for Mother's Day, and dumped aprons in a trash pile to symbolize their demand for equal rights in the marketplace. Taking more direct action, NOW brought suit against the federal government for not enforcing the sex discrimination law on behalf of women.

President Lyndon B. Johnson felt irked at Betty for forcing him to confront the issue on her terms. Reluctantly, he issued a Presidential order outlawing sex discrimination by the government and its contractors.

By 1967, Betty's crusades had become so newsworthy that five national magazines began asking her for major articles on NOW's fight against sex discrimination. As political parties prepared for a new presidential campaign, Betty called for the organization of all women into a strong voting bloc. NOW put pressure on both major parties and their candidates to support a "Bill of Rights for Women."

The 1967 NOW convention went on record supporting the ERA and the right of women to choose abortion. Some members disagreed on the abortion issue, and withdrew from NOW to organize the anti-abortion Women's Equity Action League (WEAL).

Although Betty carefully tried to keep her own politics out of NOW, she was deeply disturbed by the war in Vietnam. Marching for peace with her children, she personally supported anti–Vietnam War candidate Eugene McCarthy for president.

She attended the 1968 Democratic Convention in Chicago to help McCarthy win the presidential nomination. Witnessing the savage police riot ordered by Mayor Daley against long-haired young anti-war demonstrators, her own son among them, Betty was horrified. She ducked under the barrier protecting the press, and joined the bloodied, weeping youths in the park.

Disillusioned with a Democratic Party whose strong-arm tactics crushed McCarthy's candidacy in favor of pro-war Hubert Humphrey, Betty abstained from voting in 1968.

EIGHT

During a visit to Sweden in 1968, Betty became deeply impressed with that country's excellent child-care centers, which received wholehearted support from Sweden's young parents and their legislators. Often both parents worked part-time so they could raise their children together, while continuing their careers. In elementary school, boys as well as girls took cooking and child-care classes, while girls as well as boys took shop. All university dormitories were sexually integrated. And all these developments had occurred in just one generation.

"I learned about the possibility of a really national policy for child care when I went to Sweden," Betty told me. If Sweden could do it, she was convinced, so could the USA.

At a 1969 NOW meeting in Chicago, Betty organized the first National Abortion Rights Action League (NARAL). Some

The abortion issue split the women's movement, and remains a controversial issue today. *Above*, a pro-choice rally outside St. Patrick's Cathedral in New York City in 1989. *Below*, a group of pro-life supporters stage a counter-demonstration at the 1989 pro-choice march in Washington, DC.

women protested that abortion was not a true feminist issue. But NARAL persuaded the New York legislature to pass laws decreeing women's right to choice, and right to medical assistance.

In 1970, President Richard Nixon sought to appoint Judge Harold Carswell to a vacancy on the Supreme Court. Betty led a women's protest based on Carswell's record of sex and race discrimination, and testified against him in Congress. Joined by civil rights leaders, Betty was able to block Carswell's nomination by a Senate committee.

She was aware that many women were kept from joining NOW because of their fear of the labels "feminist" or "women's libber." For them, she initiated a Congress to Unite Women in all cities where NOW had branches. But to Betty's chagrin, radical feminists in some cities stole the headlines by using shock tactics.

Some jumped onstage at meetings to cut off all their hair and make themselves unattractive to men. Others ejected men physically from their meetings. Betty suspected that the CIA was responsible, trying to discredit the women's movement by using agents provocateurs. This was the period when President Nixon was using "dirty tricks" operatives, including FBI and CIA agents, a period that ended with the Watergate scandal and Nixon's resignation.

By this time, Betty began to feel the great strain of trying to rescue the women of America from the Feminine Mystique while keeping her own shaky marriage together. In May, 1969, she finally summoned up the courage to divorce Carl, despite warnings that this could hurt her reputation and career. "I kept my divorce as quiet as possible," she wrote, "to 'protect' the movement."

Living alone now with full custody of the children, Betty had to return to her typewriter to earn her own living. In 1970, she stepped down as president of NOW. The final act of her four-year presidency was to organize the twenty-four-hour general Women's

Strike for Equality, with marches in major US cities. Women strikers stopped work, and refused to cook or make love that night.

"It showed," Betty said, "the power of our solidarity, the power of our sisterhood."

On December 12, 1970, Betty and her colleagues again marched down Fifth Avenue, this time in a sleet storm, to demand child-care programs and abortion rights. To Betty's dismay, some radical lesbians in the march conspired to publicize it as a lesbian event, discrediting it in the eyes of most of the public.

Betty indignantly pulled out of the Women's Strike Coalition. She became distrustful of other women working in the organizations that she created, afraid that they would take them over for their own purposes. So in 1971, Betty joined *Ms.* editor Gloria Steinem and former congresswoman Bella Abzug in forming the National Women's Political Caucus (NWPC).

The new organization was aimed at increasing women's political clout by supporting candidates and judges pledged to eliminate sexism, poverty, and racism, while pressing for greater female representation in American politics. Together with NOW, the NWPC also continued the struggle to get the last three needed states to ratify the ERA as a constitutional amendment. It was tormenting to Betty to be so close to winning the battle for the ERA, only to be thwarted by the angry resistance of a few conservative state legislatures.

The following year saw women play an important role in national political conventions for the first time. Inspired by the NWPC, they forced both major parties to promise child care, pre-school, and after-school programs. Many women ran for political office, including Shirley Chisholm, who ran for the presidency. Betty herself joined ex-Congresswoman Chisholm on the campaign trail.

Bowing to pressure from Betty's organizations, the State Department now forbade officials to fire women from the foreign service when they married. In a nod to the NWPC's wry slogan, "Make policy, not coffee," officials were forbidden to force secretaries to bring them coffee. Betty's influence was also felt in churches and synagogues. Women began to be ordained as ministers, rabbis, and deacons. Non-sexist language—with God no longer referred to as "He"—was adopted for some religious services.

The NWPC was not without division. Betty found herself at odds with some feminist leaders over the troublesome question of whether the new organization should exclude men from its ranks. Betty felt that both men and women had a stake in the feminist revolution and had to work together, with women taking the lead in the fight. Her opponents insisted that it was neither practical nor possible to raise women's consciousness by working with men.

In 1970, Betty was invited by *McCall's,* then briefly edited by two feminist women editors, to write a column, "Betty Friedan's Notebook." With a readership of eight million women and the reputation of an "Establishment" magazine, *McCall's* gave Betty an ideal opportunity to spread the feminist message. The column ran for three years, greatly influencing readers to support women's liberation, until a man unsympathetic to the feminist movement replaced the women editors.

When *The Feminine Mystique* was published in Brazil, Betty was asked to go to that country to start a women's liberation movement. Her press conferences in Rio de Janeiro created a sensation. One angry newspaper editor ran a front-page editorial inviting the brassy-lunged Yankee lady to stop stirring up Brazilian women against male machismo, and go home.

Betty was the only woman invited among male celebrities to speak before the Cultural Association in Italy. When Italian women flocked to hear her at a pro-choice abortion rally in Rome, they were blocked by Fascist thugs and police. Standing on a café table to address them in pouring rain, Betty accused male political leaders of helping Italy's male neo-Fascists while ignoring the real problems of Italian women.

Betty's international prestige made her an increasing target for barbs from other less radical and envious woman writers. Her women's movement was accused of fostering "sex class warfare."

NINE

On the tenth anniversary of the publication of *The Feminine Mystique,* the NOW convention of 1973 assembled in Washington. A thousand women delegates joined hands in the hotel ballroom and began dancing in a huge circle. They sang proudly, "There is nothing I can't do. . . . I am strong. . . . I am invincible. . . . I am woman!" Addressing the convention, Betty said they were now strong enough to deal with men not as masters or oppressors, but as people they had to live, work, fight, and love with as equals.

By now the most distinguished figure in the women's movement, Betty was asked to teach at Temple University as Visiting Professor of Sociology. Later, Yale and Queens College asked her to teach "The Sex-Role Revolution, Stage II." Thanks largely to Betty, many colleges, and even high schools, began to introduce women's studies into their curricula.

As the women's movement gained power, the admission of women to medical school rose from 3 to 30 percent. Even West Point, that bastion of masculinity, began to admit women, and Betty was invited to raise the consciousness of the male West Pointers. After three days of lectures, classes, and seminars, she won many over to a new and more enlightened view of women. Lecturing at the US Air Force Academy, she also won a standing ovation from the cadets.

Betty was asked to lead consciousness-raising sessions for the trainers of guidance counselors; for priests; and even for investment bankers. Speaking to men's groups, Betty helped erase the hostility many men felt toward women's liberation by explaining the advantages derived by both men and women when they shared the work and pleasures of society equally. New polls showed even more men than women now supporting the Equal Rights Amendment, especially among younger, better-educated males.

In 1974, NOW held a Marriage and Divorce Conference which demanded enforcement machinery for child support payments. Betty admitted that she hadn't been able to collect a penny of her own child support award after five years as a divorcée. The conference also demanded Social Security for women in their own right, and "severance pay" for wives in divorce suits.

To help women further win control of their own money and exercise economic power, the First Women's Bank & Trust Company opened in October, 1975. Betty had begun organizing the bank three years earlier, and it now listed 7,000 stockholders, mostly women. The bank pledged no sex discrimination in credit, mortgages, and loans, a problem women ran into with most commercial banks.

The American Humanist Association named Betty its 1975 "Humanist of the Year." Her alma mater, Smith College, awarded her an honorary Doctorate of Human Letters. It seemed Betty had also won mainstream acceptance when she was elected to the Girl Scouts National Board. Even the Pope received Betty, awarding her a medal for her work on behalf of women, despite her advocacy of women's right to choose abortion.

Betty was able to persuade the United Nations to hold a 1975 World Conference on Women. Mexico City was chosen as the site. Months before Betty prepared to attend, she received anonymous letters warning her not to go or she would be denounced both as an unwelcome Yankee and a Jew. Betty went.

At the conference, she helped organize unofficial "global speakouts" to unite the 5,000 women delegates from all over the world. Mexican newspapers attacked Betty for allegedly insulting the president of Mexico by accusing him of machismo. Threats were made against her if she organized a woman's march.

One of Betty's meetings was broken up by male disrupters who marched into the meeting hall, shouting, pushing, and threatening the women. Another meeting was broken up by men carrying guns. Betty found herself followed everywhere by two men, and grew frightened that she would be either kidnapped or shot. Warned by a technical adviser to the US delegation that her life was really in danger, she flew back to the United States.

TEN

Despite this international setback, Betty was gratified that chapters of NOW had been founded in over seven hundred American cities, and were beginning to enjoy real power. NOW and other feminist organizations represented some 50 million Americans in support of the ERA. But pressure from the Reagan administration continued to keep the last three needed states from ratifying it, and the amendment died.

The women's movement had nevertheless brought about dramatic changes by 1976. There was now a new public image of modern women. Many TV dramas and sitcoms featured heroines who were dynamic, bright, and attractive, held professional jobs, and often led adventurous lives. More and more women appeared as TV newscasters, and in 1976, a woman became the first network vice president for TV news and public affairs.

Women were entering the training and work forces in increasing numbers, some by choice, many out of necessity, for it often took two incomes for families to keep pace with the soaring cost of living. While still assuming primary responsibility for homemaking, women no longer found it contradictory that they were also entitled to equal rights in jobs and education. Women did not have to sacrifice one for the other.

Still, Betty was aware that most families living in poverty were headed by unmarried or divorced women. Even now, working women earned barely more than half a man's salary. In 1976, Betty urged the women's movement to join forces with male labor leaders, to fight for social reforms that could benefit both male and female workers.

In 1979, Betty became chairperson of the Emergency Project for Equal Rights of NOW's Legal Defense and Education Fund. She presided over its National Assembly on the Future of the Family. The following year, she was named a delegate to the White House Conference on Families.

Twenty years after she had begun writing *The Feminine Mystique,* Betty realized that, thanks largely to her efforts, the old mystique had been toppled by women of her own generation. Most of the new generation now took women's rights and opportunities for granted. But they still had problems putting together their multifaceted roles as workers, wives, mothers, and individuals.

By 1980, the majority of American women supported the ERA. They expressed an anti-conservative viewpoint by voting against Ronald Reagan for president, who was nevertheless elected because of a 54 to 37 male vote. Women who still opposed the ERA were generally conservatives who felt threatened by women's liberation.

Eight years of the Reagan administration saw budget slashes that cut funds for enforcement of sex discrimination laws in employment and education. Government services vital to poor women such as food stamps and school lunches were whittled away. Funds for women's training programs and small business loans dried up.

The conservative thrust of the Reagan years wiped out many gains for sex equality, largely muting the women's movement, in the name of preserving traditional American family life. Betty saw this reaction as a conservative backlash against the progress of women's liberation since *The Feminine Mystique.*

In 1981, reviewing the swiftly changing scene in America, she decided that the women's movement had directed too much of its energy into a class struggle against men. She saw the need now for a "Second Stage"—regaining control over family, children, and home, while joining men in jobs, unions, companies, and professions to demand a new human control over working conditions.

Almost half the women with children under six, and two-thirds with children over six, were now in the work force. Betty saw a vital need to change the workplace to allow for maternity *and* paternity leave; parental sick leave and sabbaticals; reduced work schedules; working hour adjustments and job sharing, to permit parent care; and childcare support systems.

This "Second Stage," Betty declared, might require the support of men at the "cutting edge." Such men would have more clout to force the restructuring of American institutions so they would better serve family life, on a basis of real equality between women and men. Betty also stressed the need in the Second Stage for new approaches to divorce; abortion reform; housing and education. These policies had to be shaped in ways that would unite, not divide, women in their demands of the government and the business world.

Betty's second book, *It Changed My Life,* described how writing *The Feminine Mystique* had affected her own life, as well as the lives of the millions of women who had read the book, or read about it. Her third book, *The Second Stage,* published in 1981, described what had happened to the feminist revolution she had helped foster, and what she saw as the next direction it should take. It was a visionary look into the future for American men, women, and children, and for our changing economy and lifestyle.

I asked Betty if it was really practical to believe that a professional woman, who had stayed home to nurture her family for twenty years, could be retrained adequately in all the technological changes occurring in her field during that time.

"I think," she replied, "there should be an option for women—or men—who choose to stay home with their kids for some months or a couple of years, if they can afford it, which most people can't. Even if they could afford it, you would need some provision for the woman to get a refresher or retraining course to get back in again. But this is not insuperable. Men who spent two or three years in the armed services were returned to their professions."

The Resource Center for Non-Violence in Santa Cruz, California, revealed in 1989 that the United States ranked only sixteenth among nations for the percentage of women enrolled in universities. How did this fact, I asked her, square with Betty's expectation of specialized education for women?

"Women are today more than half the college students in this country," she replied. "They are about 40 percent of medical and law students. There's been a great increase in the number of women PhDs. True, we are a backward nation as far as certain policies are concerned, like child care and parental leave. In the Reagan-Bush era . . . there is an erosion in the rights that women have won in the last twenty years. Plus a general permission from government for sex discrimination."

Betty's belief that in the second stage of women's liberation they would need to cooperate with men, rather than oppose them, brought intense attacks from colleagues who felt that she was betraying the feminist revolution.

There are several sardonic references to Betty in a 1983 book by Gloria Steinem, *Outrageous Acts and Everyday Rebellions.* Simone de Beauvoir's book, *The Second Sex,* had made Betty's points earlier, Steinem scoffed. And she wrote, "Despite the many early reformist virtues of *The Feminist Mystique,* it had managed to appear at the height of the civil rights movement with almost no reference to black women or other women of color."

Betty was also under attack from the Right by women conservatives who still believed in the Feminine Mystique that she had shattered. Disheartened by the attacks upon her, in 1982 she retreated to Harvard as a Fellow of the Institute of Politics of the Kennedy School of Government. She also joined the faculty of the Department for the Study of Women and Men in Society at the University of Southern California. But she remained active in pursuit of her vision that the women's movement had to enter and win the Second Stage.

Her creations, NOW and the NWPC, continued to be powerful forces behind the feminist revolution all through the eighties.

I asked Betty what her next projects were.

"The book that I'm working on now," she told me, "goes beyond those questions. It's going to be called *The Fountain of Age.* I am now applying to the question of women and age everything I learned about women, about breaking through the Feminine Mystique, about what I learned of the Second Stage.

"The mystique of age is devastating for both women and men. I will apply everything I learned to the possibilities of this unique period of life after the child-bearing, child-rearing years, to make them years of true human fruition and maturity."

We haven't heard the last of Betty Friedan or the sweeping changes she has made, and will yet make, in the way all of us, not only women, live.

The Feminist
Revolution Tomorrow

ONE

Women have made great progress in the twentieth century toward independence from and equality with men. Susan Anthony would scarcely believe the remarkable changes in women's lives that have taken place from her day to this. Women today enjoy the right to vote; to run for public office; to achieve PhDs; to pursue professional careers; to compete for top positions in the economic world; and to enter such formerly male-only occupations as police officers, firefighters, linesmen, coal miners, truckers, doctors, electricians, soldiers, lawyers, judges, and governors.

But much still remains to be done before women can be said to have achieved full equality with men.

One major problem facing today's career women is exemplified in a letter Betty Friedan received from a young woman in her third year at Harvard Medical School. "I'll never be a trapped housewife like my mother," it vowed. "But I would like to get married and have children, I think. They say we can have it all. But how? I work thirty-six hours in the hospital, twelve off. How am I going to have a relationship, much less kids with hours like that? I'm not sure I can be a superwoman . . . Either I won't be able to have the kind of marriage I dream of or the kind of medical career I want."

The problems faced by working women with children are not exactly new. At the turn of the century, feminist Charlotte Perkins Gilman declared that not only did women have the right to employment, but that society would have to make it possible for them to balance the demands of child rearing and work. Almost a century later, that problem still requires solutions.

The Labor Department reveals that 70 percent of women aged twenty-five to thirty-four are in the work force today, compared to only 35 percent in 1950. And over half are mothers with children under six. More than ten million pre-school children have mothers in the work force. By 1995, this number will increase to fifteen million. The problem of child care for working mothers is a serious and growing one.

A few progressive companies do now provide child care for employees, but they are the exceptions. "For too many Americans," points out Senator William C. Cohen, a Maine Republican, "lack of affordable, quality day care becomes an obstacle to education, employment, or training for employment." A quarter of America's sixty-three million children live with only one parent, usually the mother, and such households have a poverty rate of 55 percent. An Illinois study reported in the *Moline Dispatch* found that "only one in seven Illinois children who needs low-income child care gets it now. About 100,000 under the age of six need the service."

A bill allowing new parents unpaid parental leave from their jobs for up to ten weeks, and guaranteeing their jobs, has been pending in Congress since 1985. Business lobbyists have held it up, meanwhile watering down the bill so that companies with less than fifty employees would not be covered. In 1990, the House passed the bill, but President Bush indicated he would veto it if the Senate passed it.

Proposals have been made to give working parents tax credits and vouchers for child care. But columnist Jack Anderson raised the question, "Then don't stay-at-home parents deserve the same? After all, they are the ones without the paycheck."

I asked Betty Friedan her opinion.

"I would like to see national policies on parental leave, about which our country is very remiss," she told me. "We're a backward nation. We are the only nation outside of South Africa without national policies of parental leave and child care. Countries like Australia have a very decent period of paid parental leave. People can take three years, and in some instances seven years and are able to go back to their jobs."

She added, "As a matter of simple economic reality, it is really not possible for women in this country to take off any number of years, certainly the way it is now. Their income is necessary, given the cost of housing and school tuition, and the rest of it, and the way the professions are structured. There is no provision that guarantees that if women take off very long, they can get back in a meaningful level."

One Seattle woman wrote columnist Ann Landers: "I, too, stayed home to raise three children, and tried to get back in the work force when our youngest went to high school. I had dozens of interviews, but nobody would hire me. I knew it was my age. Finally I offered my services to a senior citizens' group. They said, 'Sorry, you're too young.'"

Despite laws against sex discrimination, it is still very much present in the workplace. On the average, women are still paid only sixty-four cents for every dollar earned by men. And although more careers are being opened to women, achieving top positions remains one of the most difficult struggles for tomorrow's feminists.

Already, in many industries women have been able to move up the ladder of promotions, possibly because a third of all Master of Business Administration graduates today are women. Yet there isn't one woman running the top one hundred companies cited by *Forbes* magazine.

"American business is very much a white male arena," charges Susan King, president of Steuben Glass. "The deck has been stacked against women." Wendy Reid Crisp, president of the National Association of Female Executives, adds, "When the chips are down, men get the jobs."

Ann Hopkins filed suit in 1982 against Price-Waterhouse for denying her a partnership despite her having the best record among eighty-eight candidates, all men, for the post. Male partners told her she was too "macho," needed "a course in charm school," had to walk and dress more femininely and wear makeup and jewelry. In 1989, the Supreme Court ruled that the firm had been guilty of "unlawful stereotyping." But at the same time the Court made it more difficult for women to prove discrimination.

The Supreme Court, restructured by the appointments of Republican presidents Richard Nixon, Ronald Reagan, and George Bush, is accused by the women's movement of attempts to weaken laws forbidding sex discrimination. The Court's rulings made it more difficult for women to prove on-the-job bias; facts such as that no woman received one of a company's forty promotions can no longer be used as evidence. It also gave men power to challenge affirmative action laws fostering female equality as "reverse discrimination" against men.

"The Court's record," declared Norman Dorsent, president of the American Civil Liberties Union, "was the worst in decades."

Some women oppose reforms to guarantee women equal treatment in the workplace. Felice Schwartz, president of Catalyst, a women's business research group, created a furor with her article expressing this viewpoint in the *Harvard Business Review.*

She argued that women managers must be considered differently from men managers because many eventually have children, and leave or cut back on work commitments for infant care. Companies therefore lose the money spent training them. Schwartz suggested that companies should establish a "mommy track" which would distinguish between "career primary" women who would put work first, and therefore should be groomed for top jobs, and "career and family women." The latter would be offered part-time jobs and flexible hours.

The issue is an important one because women will make up two-thirds of the incoming work force by the year 2000, according to Department of Labor estimates; that includes 84 percent of all women of childbearing years.

Supporters of Felice Schwartz insist that we need to establish flexible career paths for women to permit them to function both as business executives and mothers.

But opponents stress that the "mommy track" is discriminatory. By describing children as women's sole responsibility, the path to promotions is being closed to them. Opponents insist instead that business must set up flexible job options for *both* parents. Representative Pat Schroeder prefers solutions that address the problem of *family,* not of women alone, such as company-funded child care and parental leave.

University of Texas psychologist Lucia A. Gilbert protested, "My fear is that if only women take this option, they won't move up the career ladder and they have a guaranteed position as the primary parent. We'll be back where we were in the '60s."

Ann Leibowitz, legal counsel for the Polaroid Corporation, also pointed out, "The more employers make special provisions for women, the more they find reasons not to hire them."

While laws on the books prohibit employers from discriminating against women because of their sex, there are none preventing them from refusing women employment because of age. Career women complain that TV news networks discriminate against women who are considered too old or not pretty. News anchorwoman Christine Craft went to court charging that she was fired because of age discrimination. CBS promoted Connie Chung to be a TV news anchorwoman at a salary of close to two million dollars a year. But she declared wryly, "You'll know when women have really made it on TV when you see a top woman newscaster who looks like David Brinkley!"

Lou Glasse, president of the Older Women's League, reported that seven out of ten women aged sixty-five or older are poor. One reason is that there are few jobs for women over fifty.

This problem will grow increasingly important in the decades ahead as the elderly American population increases in size. Employers themselves may be eager to change their negative attitude toward women over fifty because there will be fewer young workers available in tomorrow's population to fill all the jobs. But until this demographic change takes place, feminists will continue to press for laws against discrimination because of age, as well as because of gender.

TWO

A woman's right to choose abortion has been guaranteed since 1973 by the Supreme Court's decision in *Roe* v. *Wade*. But the new Rehnquist Court undercut that ruling by giving each state legislature the right to amend or reverse it. Each state that did so would, in effect, be denying its poor women the right of choice. In response, the women's movement organized the largest protest march in Washington's history.

Three hundred thousand people gathered for the April, 1989, demonstration. The *New York Times* reported that "the presence of mothers and daughters together" at the protest was notable. Their signs read: MY BODY, MY BABY, MY BUSINESS, and KEEP YOUR LAWS OFF MY BODY. The feminists pointed out that every year more than 200,000 deaths from illegal abortions were reported around the world. But where abortion was legal, only one in 200,000 women died from the procedure.

The anti-abortion Right to Life movement rejoiced in the new Supreme Court decision. Phyllis Schlafly, president of the anti-feminist Eagle Forum, declared, "Women have babies and men provide the support. If you don't like the way we're made you've got to take it up with God." The Right to Life organization also sought to block testing and distribution in the United States of a newly developed French pill called RU-486, which expelled the ovum after conception may have taken place, as opposed to the birth control pill which prevented conception. To Right to Lifers, the fertilized ovum represented human life from the moment of conception.

Right to Lifers were further incensed when Reagan-appointed Surgeon General Dr. C. Everett Koop issued a report endorsing abortion. He also warned, "children who cannot be cared for by the mother or her parents place demands on the state for welfare services and financial support." Dr. Koop's violation of Reagan's anti-feminist orientation infuriated anti-abortion conservatives who whipped up a political storm of protest and demanded Dr. Koop's ouster.

The Children's Defense Fund found that pregnancy was six times more likely among teenagers who are poor and lack basic economic skills. In 1986, 61 percent of teenage births were out of wedlock. An estimated one in five children in the United States today lives in poverty.

Nevertheless, the Right to Life movement vowed to defeat any legislator who refused to vote against abortion. I asked Betty Friedan how she felt about one-issue politics—voting for or against a candidate depending alone on his or her stand for or against free choice of abortion for women.

"Abortion isn't a single issue," she replied. "We cannot allow our constitutional rights to privacy, and the choice to control our reproductive process, to be eroded. This is a basic issue. And it is connected with other issues. Woman's economic survival requires that she be allowed to decide when, whether, and how many times to bear a child; to have access to birth control; and the choice of abortion.

"Furthermore," she added, "if the Supreme Court undermines the entire principle of constitutional protection for women, in terms of the right of privacy and the question of abortion, the next thing we'll do it on is birth control. Or on women's right to equal opportunity, which is already being eroded by the previous Supreme Court decision on affirmative action. So in that sense it is not a narrow single issue. It is a basic issue."

Betty met with friends and neighbors to plan a rally in defense of women's constitutional rights to privacy and abortion choice. All the elected representatives in the area of her summer home were opposed to those rights. So Betty proposed that voters' pledge cards be sent to them stating, "I will not vote for you unless you vote pro-choice."

"With the Supreme Court no longer there to protect our constitutional rights," Betty told me, "it becomes a matter of state legislative and congressional decision. So we cannot support any congressman or state legislator who opposes women's right of choice, because this right is basic to the personhood of women."

THREE

The Equal Rights Amendment has still not been ratified by all the necessary states. Opposition has come from conservative women's groups who oppose the feminist movement. In a book called *Women of the Right*, Professor Rebecca Klatch declares that what feminists consider emancipation, socially conservative women regard as disintegration of the family.

Right-wing conservatives of both sexes are disturbed by the growing number of women in the workplace, regardless of the need for the income. They view this development as threatening to family life.

"I listen to feminists and all these radical gals—most of them failures," declared Rev. Jerry Falwell, founder of the now-defunct Moral Majority. "They've blown it. Some of them have been married, but they married some Casper Milquetoast who asked permission to go to the bathroom. These women just need a man in the house. That's all they need. Most of these feminists need a man to tell them what time of day it is and to lead them home. And they blew it and they're mad at all men. Feminists hate men. They're sexist. They hate men—that's their problem."

Many young men today don't agree. Most appreciate the economic help of their wives' salaries in meeting today's high cost of living. Some studies show that young husbands now do twice the amount of housework they performed in 1965.

Nevertheless, in her book, *The Second Shift*, Berkeley professor of sociology Arlie Hochschild reports that most working women today work two full shifts—one at the workplace, and one at home. Working wives labor an average fifteen hours longer every week than their husbands, who offer little, if any, help with household and infant care chores.

I asked Betty Friedan if she believed it was possible for young working parents to put their lifestyle together successfully without a reduction of working hours.

"They're doing it," she replied. "There are many reasons to believe from research that the quality of family life, where both parents work and share the responsibilities of the children, is superior to the traditional family. It is harassing especially for the mother, however, because she is also doing full-time work while still considered to have the main responsibility for the children."

She advocates a new kind of housing which could provide privacy, but at the same time offer some sharing of services like laundry, child care, meal preparation, dining room, and social activities. She found such "service housing" in Sweden. This kind of housing, Betty believes, would help couples and single parents with children to pursue their careers, while economizing the time demands made on them by housework and child care.

Professor Hochschild, too, cites the example of Sweden, which a 1990 UN survey found to have the world's highest standard of living. Sweden subsidizes a wide range of services to help working parents, from daycare centers to eighteen months of paid maternity and paternity leave. But Sweden nevertheless has a problem in persuading new fathers to take advantage of that leave. Only 6 percent do.

"That Daddy stays home is still not seen as really natural," reports Birgitta Finnander, an electrical engineering student in

Lundkoping. And Kjell Post, a Swedish computer science graduate, explains, "Because men still hold most of the high-paying
positions, families might not be able to maintain the same standard of living if they have to live on the mother's salary and the
paternity leave insurance. . . . [Also] if a person has been on leave
for a long time, he might not have the same chance to get a high
position in his field."

But there are signs that future American husbands may be
more willing to share home tasks with their wives. Many boys
are joining the Future Homemakers of America, which was
formerly perceived as a girls' organization encouraging home
economic skills. Accordingly, the organization is considering
changing its name to accommodate the boys among its 285,000
student members.

Professor Hochschild points out that the one thing she found
that contributed most to marital happiness was "the husband's
willingness to do the work at home."

Phyllis Schlafly objects strenuously to the presentation of the
feminist viewpoint in American classrooms. In her book *Child
Abuse in the Classroom*, she deplored "the radical notion of a
gender-free society in which there are no differences in attitude
and occupations between men and women." She protested against
school library materials that "induce role reversals by showing
women in hard physical labor jobs and men as house husbands."

Such viewpoints illustrate the persistent ultra-conservative
belief in the Feminine Mystique that Betty Friedan destroyed.

FOUR

The law's protection of women from male abuse still leaves
much to be desired. The World Watch Institute, a Washington-
based research group, reports that violence against women is a
widespread, yet largely ignored, problem. "Women are targets of
violence because of their sex," Lori Heise wrote in the *Washing-*

ton *Post.* "This is not random violence. The risk factor is being female."

In the United States, declared former Surgeon General Koop, as many as fifteen million women have been beaten, raped, or have suffered other forms of physical and sexual assault, with the number rising by as much as a million per year.

In 1990, educators were disturbed by what seemed to be a rising incidence of sexual harassment on college campuses. Incidents ranged from molestation to rape, and even in some bizarre cases, to kidnapping and torture.

"For many of us," says Hedy Nuriel, vice chairperson of the National Coalition of Domestic Violence, "it's safer to be out on the streets than in our own homes."

President George Bush declared in June, 1989, that "archaic and unacceptable" attitudes toward women help breed violent crimes against them, and rob them of full equality in American life. This "climate of fear" made them afraid to work late or walk to a library at night. "This war against women must stop," the president told a convention of the American Association of University Women.

Divorced women today still find serious inequalities in their lives after separation from husbands. For a long time, divorced husbands dodged paying court-ordered support for their children simply by skipping to another state. To enforce payment, new laws permitted ex-wives to garnishee the salaries of their ex-husbands across state boundaries. But most ex-husbands still manage to remain conveniently "lost."

Divorce settlements have proved so inadequate that sociologist Lenore J. Weitzman, in her book, *The Divorce Revolution,* revealed that divorced women and their children suffer an immediate drop of 73 percent in their standard of living, while the ex-husbands enjoy a 42 percent rise in theirs.

Many women in church-related positions today still find it an uphill battle to fight sex discrimination. Mary Daly was an associate professor of theology at Jesuit-run Boston College for twenty years. Turned down for promotion twice, she was severely criticized for her lack of "traditional" scholarship.

Professor Daly's crime was her contention that the entire system of Christian symbols was inherently oppressive to women. "For a radical feminist to try to change the church," she said, "was like a black person trying to reform the Ku Klux Klan."

A furor in the religious community was stirred when the Reverend Barbara Harris was made a bishop of the Episcopal Church. Despite the fact that the United Methodist Church had already elected five women bishops, there was heated controversy among Episcopalians over the spiritual equality of women.

"Christian feminists," one disgusted Ohio woman wrote *Newsweek,* "are fighting a losing battle."

For a long while, women have been familiar figures riding on motorcycles behind a male driver. But because motorcycles are one of the cheapest forms of transportation available, with low insurance rates and easy parking, more and more women have taken to driving motorcycles on their own. Many report, however, a lot of verbal harassment from male car drivers, who seem to resent seeing women driving what traditionally has been thought of as a vehicle for males.

Shelley Lovelance of Albuquerque, New Mexico, who rides a Yamaha 250 Exciter, finds that she can ignore the abuse while she's driving. "But when I'm sitting still, when I'm buying gas, when I'm parking or getting out of a parking space, I really feel vulnerable."

Prejudice against women also extends to school libraries. A survey by the Center for the Learning & Teaching of Literature at State University of New York at Albany found that only one of the ten most frequently assigned books in public and private high schools was written by a woman—Harper Lee's *To Kill A Mockingbird.* And none was written by a minority author.

"This," pointed out survey director Arthur N. Applebee, "two decades after the civil rights and women's movements focused national attention on imbalances and inequities in the school curriculum."

Feminists were also chagrined to find that, despite women's consciousness-raising gains of the last few decades, most TV commercials watched by children today still perpetuate sexist stereotypes. Boys are still depicted playing sports and being rowdy, while girls play with Barbie-type dolls that are offered with accessories such as nail polish, makeup, perfume, and blonde wigs.

"The disservice to society noted back in 1968 is still very much with us," observed John J. O'Connor in *The New York Times* under the headline KIDS' TV ADS; WORSE THAN EVER. He added, "The time has probably arrived for another national debate."

In pursuit of her goal of changing sexist portrayals of women in the media, feminist Ann Simonton organized Media Watch in 1984. To improve the media image of women nationally and internationally, members are alerted to write protests against offending TV programs, newspapers, or magazines. Media Watch has sister groups in Canada, Australia, and Japan.

"We are trying to empower women to overcome the media stereotypes and help define themselves," Simonton declares. "The media has distorted our reality. We need to create a new honest reality that reflects the feminist point of view."

FIVE

Computers will have an important place in the lives of women tomorrow. Joyce Hakansson, a Berkeley educator who founded a software company to develop programs for children, observed, "There doesn't seem to be real differences between young girls and young boys in either their math ability or their ability to enjoy computers. . . . [But] When girls get to be junior high school age, it's not cool to be good at calculations or computation and things that are empowering."

In 1984, Harvard researchers studying 55,000 elementary and high school students found that three out of four enrolled in computer camps were boys. Parents, the researchers learned, were willing to spend significantly more money to send their sons than their daughters to these camps.

"We found that in general women started out behind," reported Dr. Sara Kiesler, a psychologist at Camegie-Mellon University, one of the nation's leading computer science centers. "They had no summer jobs, no computer camp, and no experience in high school with computers." As a result, males were far more experienced with computers at the college level than females. This made it harder for women to compete with men for prime jobs on an equal basis.

Looking ahead to the place of women in tomorrow's world around the globe, the UN. Population Fund predicted in its 1989 World Population Report that unless women win more access to family planning, education, and employment, the world's population could almost triple to fourteen billion by the year 2100.

In half the countries where cultural values put men first, women have no access to family planning services. An explosive world birthrate could result in starvation for hundreds of millions of people in countries with inadequate food resources.

The Planned Parenthood Federation of America is the largest volunteer organization in the world after the Red Cross. Its clinics provide the opportunity for over 200 million women to control their fertility. They offer high quality, low-cost health care and education for all who need and request it.

As a result, less than 5 percent of their services include abortion. Planned Parenthood has helped nations with teeming populations like India, Pakistan, and China to control their birthrates through contraceptive programs. Yet despite this invaluable work, conservatives have succeeded in getting the government to block international funds for Planned Parenthood's work overseas. The pro-life movement has also tried to shut down its clinics with "Operation Rescue" demonstrations, and has threatened corporations which did not end their contributions to Planned Parenthood.

Dread of an accidental nuclear war still worries American women and their children, despite vastly improved relations between the US and the USSR. Their fears were not eased by the world conflict over Iraq's invasion of Kuwait in 1990. "There are about 20 million children in this country under the age of 12," wrote Erma Bombeck, "and do you know what worries them most? They're worried that nuclear war may keep them from turning into teenagers. They don't talk about it a lot, but in a poll an unsettling 44 percent of them listed it as their No. 1 concern."

Moved by these fears, women have organized to write letters, circulate petitions, and talk to congressmen about the imperative need for peace and disarmament. Women's organizations like Women's Strike for Peace, Grandmothers for Peace, and the Gray Panthers have demonstrated against our military buildup.

"War is obsolete," states the Women's Peace Platform of Women for a Meaningful Summit. "The existence of nuclear and conventional weapons is not a source of security. We are not the enemies of one another. Our real enemies are hunger, disease, racism, poverty, inequality, injustice, and violence."

Although American women, like those in every major and almost all smaller nations, now enjoy the vote, there are still a few places in the world where women do not. Until 1989, even in Switzerland two cantons denied woman suffrage. Then the men in one canton, Appenzell Outer-Rhodes, decided by a show of hands to give women the vote. "I can look my wife in the eye again," one townsman told the Associated Press. But Swiss women still can't vote in the neighboring canton of Appenzell Inner-Rhodes.

Women in Japan have the vote, but continue to live as second-class citizens in a masculine world. In July, 1989, Agriculture Minister Hisao Horinouchi declared that women were useless in politics and should stay home. "In the end," he said, "women's task is to stay home and take care of their families."

Socialist Party chairwoman Takako Doi, campaigning for office, declared herself "flabbergasted" by Horinouchi's chauvinism. Michiko Matsuura, head of the Japan League of Women Voters, told the Associated Press, "Women are going to react against this when they vote." Taken aback by a firestorm of female opposition, Horinouchi hastily declared, "I deeply apologize for having made remarks that have bothered so many women. I would like to retract them completely." But the Socialist Party, led by a woman, scored a victory in Tokyo's municipal elections, tripling their strength from twelve seats to thirty-six.

In the United States, NOW ended its 1989 convention by announcing that it would explore the possibility of forming a new political party for women, dedicated to achieving equality. NOW president Molly Yard declared that her members felt "total disgust" with the Democratic and Republican parties for their failure to address women's needs.

"We are 52 percent of the country," Yard pointed out, "and we have almost no representation. As a whole, the majority is voting against women all the time. We're sick of it."

NOW proposed to work hard to elect more women to public office at every level—local, county, state, and federal. A NOW bumper sticker read: A WOMAN'S PLACE IS IN THE HOUSE—AND THE SENATE.

NOW's convention adopted a "Bill of Rights for the 21st Century." Demands included freedom from discrimination on the basis of race, sex, sexual orientation, or age; freedom from government interference in abortion or birth control; the right of women to receive public funds for abortions, birth control, and pregnancy services; and the right to a safe environment, a decent standard of living, and freedom from violence.

"We're fighting for women's individual rights," Yard explained. "I feel we are in a battle . . . but it's also clear we have a lot of recruits."

Betty Friedan notes that 90 percent of the world's governments have set up national bodies for the advancement of women, mostly during the last decade, while those in the United States have been dismantled. "Even Kenya," she observes, "has an equal rights clause in its Constitution!"

A *New York Times* poll in 1989 found that 67 percent of a cross section of women polled agreed that the United States "continues to need a strong women's movement to push for changes that benefit women." The women's movement was supported more ardently by women who worked outside the home than by those who did not. The *Times* noted that "the workings of the economy and feminist ideas have radically transformed the way men and women organize their work and family lives."

But a *Times* poll later that year found that 56 percent of women polled complained that American society had still not changed enough to let women compete with men on an equal basis. And careers were uppermost in the minds of today's young women.

Shannon Gilliland, eighteen, was raised with traditional values in Ludlow, Missouri. But she declared, "Our idea of home life no longer is leaving high school to get married and pregnant. We want a career, not just to be a homemaker."

More and more of today's young men accept the idea of sexual equality. Aware of many couples' need for a second paycheck to make ends meet, they are willing to support feminist demands. At the same time, more and more feminists are conscious of their need today for male support of those demands.

No longer seeing men as "the enemy," they are determined to strive for better family and work lifestyles for both sexes.

The history of the women's movement has been one of slow and steady progress, with periods of setbacks and periods of accomplishments. After the big suffrage drive ended successfully in 1920, a political backlash turned the reform movement away from women's issues to peace and arbitration efforts. In the '30s, the need to cope with Depression issues put social reform on the back burner. But in the '40s, women's role in the war effort once more led to advances for their cause. The decades since have continued to bring both victories and defeats.

Susan B. Anthony, Margaret Sanger, and Betty Friedan overcame tremendous obstacles to develop the women's movement. Their accomplishments in times much more repressive than our own suggest hope for the future of the feminist movement. As the immense April, 1989, march on Washington proved, there is a whole generation of women ready to take up the struggle for total sexual equality. As we move into the twenty-first century, we will undoubtedly see new heroines emerge in the female revolution.

Bibliography and Suggested Further Reading

(Suggested further reading indicated by *)

* Archer, Jules. *The Incredible Sixties: The Stormy Years That Changed America*. San Diego, New York, London: Harcourt Brace Jovanovich, Inc., 1986.

———. *The Unpopular Ones*. New York: Crowell-Collier Press, 1968.

* Beard, Mary R. *Woman as Force in History*. New York: Collier Books, 1962.

* Blashfield, Jean F. *Hellraisers, Heroines and Holy Women*. New York: St. Martin's Press, 1981.

* Bloomer, D. C. *Life and Writings of Amelia Bloomer*. New York: Schocken Books, 1975.

Clark, Electra. *Leading Ladies*. New York: Stein and Day Publishers, 1976.

* Dash, Joan. *A Life of One's Own*. New York, Evanston, San Francisco, London: Harper & Row, Publishers, Inc., 1973.

* Douglas, Emily Taft. *Margaret Sanger: Pioneer of the Future*. New York, Chicago, San Francisco: Holt, Rinehart and Winston, 1970.

* DuBois, Ellen Carol, ed. *Elizabeth Cady Stanton/Susan B. Anthony*. New York: Schocken Books, Inc., 1981.

*Duvall, Elizabeth S. *Hear Me For My Cause. Selected Letters of Margaret Sanger*. Northampton, MA: Smith College Press, 1967.

Flexner, Elinor. *Century of Struggle*. New York: Atheneum Publishers, 1972.

* Friedan, Betty. *The Feminine Mystique*. (20th Anniversary Edition). New York: Dell Publishing, 1984.

* ———. *It Changed My Life*. New York: Dell Publishing, 1977.

* Gray, Dorothy. *Margaret Sanger*. New York: Marek Publishers, 1979.

*Harper, Ida H. *The Life and Work of Susan B. Anthony*. Vols. I, II, III. Indianapolis: The Hollenbeck Press, 1898/1908.

*Hole, Judith & Ellen Levine. *Rebirth of Feminism*. New York: A *New York Times* Company: Quadrangle Books, 1971.

Kennedy, David M. *Birth Control in America: The Career of Margaret Sanger*. New Haven, CT and London: Yale University Press, 1970.

*Lader, Lawrence. *The Margaret Sanger Story and the Fight for Birth Control*. Garden City, NY: Doubleday & Company, 1973.

Lutz, Alena. *Susan B. Anthony: Rebel, Crusader, Humanitarian*. Washington, DC: Zenger Pub. Co., Inc., 1959.

Millett, Kate. *Sexual Politics*. New York: Doubleday & Company, 1970.

*Nies, Judith. *Seven Women: Portraits from the American Radical Tradition*. New York: The Viking Press, 1977.

*Parker, Gail, ed. *The Oven Birds: American Women on Womanhood* 1820–1920. Garden City, NY: Doubleday & Company, Inc., 1972.

*Sanger, Margaret. *An Autobiography*. New York: W.W. Norton & Company, 1938.

_____. *Happiness in Marriage*. New York: Blue Ribbon Books, 1926.

*_____. *My Fight for Birth Control*. Elmsford, NY: Maxwell Reprint Company, 1969.

_____. *Woman and the New Race*. Truth Publishing Co., 1920.

Schlafly, Phyllis. *The Power of the Positive Woman*. New Rochelle, NY: Arlington House Publishers, 1977.

*Steinem, Gloria. *Outrageous Acts* and *Everyday Rebellions*. New York: Holt, Rinehart and Winston, 1983.

*Stephenson, June. *Women's Roots*. Napa, CA: Diemer, Smith Publishing Company, Inc., 1985.

Topalian, Elyse. *Margaret Sanger*. New York, London, Toronto, Sydney: Franklin Watts, 1984.

Vance, Marguerite. *The Lamplighters: Women in the Hall of Fame*. New York: E. P. Dutton & Co., Inc., 1960.

Also consulted were articles in issues of *AARP Bulletin, ACLU News, American Way, City On a Hill, Civil Liberties, Focus on the Family, The Historian, Modern Maturity, Newsweek, The New York Times Magazine,*

Reader's Digest, San Francisco Examiner, San Jose Mercury, Santa Cruz Sentinel, Scholastic Update, Time, USA Weekend, Variety, The Washington Spectator, and Working Woman.

Personal interviews were held with Betty Friedan and Ann Simonton.

ABOUT THE AUTHOR

Jules Archer was one of the most respected names in nonfiction for young readers, with more than seventy books published. Intensive research and firsthand reporting are his hallmarks. Mr. Archer lived in Santa Cruz, California.

Index

Julian, George W., 46

Junior Leagues, 100

Kennard, Joyce, 17

Kenya, 165

Kenyon, Dorothy, 111

Kiesler, Dr. Sara, 162

King, Susan, 151

Kirby, Georgianna, 8

Klatch, Rebecca, 156

Knowlton, Dr. Charles, 78

Koop, Dr. C. Everett, 154, 155, 159

Ku Klux Klan, 160

Kuwait, 163

Labor Department, 149

Ladies Home Journal, 61, 122, 127, 128

Landers, Ann, 151

Lawrence textile strike, 72

Lee, Harper, 160

Leibowitz, Ann, 153

Lenroot, Katherine, 101

Lesbians, 132, 138

Lewis, Burdette, 88

The Lily, 32

Lincoln, Abraham, 41, 42

Lindsay, Mayor John, 111

Lin, Yutang, 101

Lippmann, Walter, 81, 83

Literary Guild Children's Book Club, 115

Little League, 13

Little Women (Alcott), 115

Lovelance, Shelley, 160

Lynd, Robert and Helen, 116

Lysistrata (Aristophanes), 3, 109

MacArthur, Gen. Douglas, 101–102

Magazine censorship, 128

Marital discontent, 113, 121, 123

Marriage, 27, 34, 39, 41, 44, 47, 49, 55, 66, 69, 70, 74, 75, 78, 79, 121, 122, 125, 137, 149

Marriage and Divorce Conference, 141

Married Women's Property Law, 31

Maternal and infant death rates, 69, 79–80

Matsuura, Michiko, 164

McCall's, 122, 127, 139

McCarran, Senator Pat, 98

McCarthy, Senator Eugene, 135

McCarthy, Senator Joseph, 120

McCormick, Kate, 104

McLean, Aaron, 26

Mead, Margaret, 126

Media, portrayals of women in, 12, 14, 113, 120, 124, 128, 129, 132, 161

Media Watch, 161

Medical schools, 7, 140, 149

Men, new role for, 139–142, 144, 145, 149, 158

Menninger, Dr. Karl, 90

Men's groups, 141

Men's magazines, 15

Menstruation, 5

Middletown (Lynd, R. and H.), 116

Miller, Elizabeth Smith, 7

Millett, Kate, 12, 111

Miss America Pageant, 12, 14

Mob attacks, 31, 34, 36, 41, 102

Molestation, 159